LEARNING TO LEAP

A guide to being more employable

David Shindler

Learning To Leap – A Guide To Being More Employable
©David Shindler

ISBN: 978-1-906316-84-6

Published in 2011 by HotHive Books, Evesham, UK.
www.thehothive.com

A CIP record of this book is available from the British Library.

Printed in the UK by TJ International, Padstow.

Dedicated to

Cath, Bex, Anna and Beth

Happy Leaving!
Best wishes

David.

Contents

Acknowledgements

I would like to thank the following people who have helped me in various ways through the hugely enjoyable experience of giving birth to my first book. In alphabetical order, they are:

Tom Beaney, Oliver Burkeman, Lily Child, Richard Child, Dan Davies, Cathy Dean, Sara Drinkwater, Chris Gardner, Helen Jones, Neil Munz-Jones, Anna Shindler, Cath Shindler, Clare Smithson, Jon Smithson, Karen Swinden, Clive Wilson.

The Rainbow

My heart leaps up when I behold
A rainbow in the sky:
So was it when my life began,
So is it now I am a man,
So be it when I shall grow old,
Or let me die!
The child is father of the man:
I could wish my days to be
Bound each to each by natural piety.

William Wordsworth (1802)

Introduction

A leap into the unknown

Imagine you are a circus trapeze artist. You have climbed up a 30-foot ladder and find yourself standing on a very small platform holding a trapeze. Opposite is a similar platform and trapeze. You really want to get to the other side. You see hard ground in between with no safety net and all eyes are watching you. You know that achieving your goal means holding on tight to the trapeze, jumping off and then letting go.

Do you freeze at the top of the ladder, afraid to let go and take that first step?

Do you jump off with confidence or trepidation?

For a brief moment there is nothing to hold you up other than your forward momentum until you can grab the other trapeze.

Are you caught in that moment between letting go and grabbing hold of the future?

Have you caught the other trapeze but found it feels unfamiliar, while being comfortably on the other platform seems like a long way away?

This book helps you close the gap between where you are now in your working life and where you want to be. Right now it can feel like taking a leap into the unknown and it feels risky. *Learning to Leap* will give you the confidence, authority and skill to jump with relish.

Lost in translation

If I were your prospective or current employer and asked you to answer the following questions at this moment in your life, could you do so confidently and authentically?

▸ What kind of person are you?

▸ What is really important to you in your life?

▸ What are you good at?

▸ How have your strengths shaped your achievements to date?

▸ What gets the best out of you?

▸ What do you struggle with? How do you deal with setbacks?

▸ What have you tried in order to improve yourself? What works for you?

▸ How do you manage yourself so you are able to be at your best more of the time?

▸ How aware are you of other people and situations?

▸ What impact do you have on other people?

▸ How well do you manage your relationships with other people?

If you can, are you then able to translate your answers into what employers want, such as:

▸ working well in a team?

▸ communicating clearly?

▸ listening well?

▸ having a 'can do' attitude?

▸ being keen to learn?

▸ taking criticism?

▸ solving problems?

▸ understanding the wants and needs of customers?

This book is about finding the 'sweet spot' – the common ground between your unique offer as a person and what an employer needs.

(with thanks to Nancy Ancowitz, business communication coach and author of *Self-Promotion for Introverts®*)

> **You can teach a bubbly person to repair shoes but you can't put the personality into a grumpy cobbler**
>
> John Timpson, Chairman of Timpsons

What is in the book?

Learning To Leap is full of tools, techniques, approaches, ideas and resources for helping you to be more employable and make the best of who you are. It explains what employers from any sector are seeking from their prospective and existing employees and how you can demonstrate your value. Inevitably, it is selective. The focus here is not on technical or subject expertise but on what you bring as a person.

You will find something here to support and maintain your employability or that of others, whatever your circumstances or age.

This book is *not* primarily about finding a job or career, although you will find helpful ideas. There is recognition that jobs are scarce and the marketplace is highly competitive. It's more about understanding and developing core personal foundations that will give you a better chance of being more employable throughout your working life. It's either a starting or renewal point depending on your situation. So it's not a quick fix, although there are some ideas you can apply straight away. Note that the book is not aimed at those with basic skills needs around literacy and numeracy, nor does it focus on being self-employed. It is aimed at people who are prospective or existing employees.

The three stages common to the development process outlined in the book are:

Getting it right
Diagnosing who you are as a person

Doing it well
Skilfully applying what you know about yourself

Making it stick
Continually learning and growing

How to use the book

To get the best out of the book, see it as a critical friend who both asks you the tough questions and gives you supportive guidance. Like a personal fitness trainer, it will put you through your paces leaving you energised and raring to go. Put the work in and you will reap the benefits. An accompanying workbook is available from www.employabilitycoaching.co.uk/resources (see Appendix 1).

Feel free to dip in and out or focus on the issue that matters to you. As an added bonus, you can keep going back at any life stage to the ideas in *Learning to Leap* and achieve even more in the future. Are you ready to take the LEAP?

> **To be employed is to be at risk, to be employable is to be secure**
>
> Dr P Hawkins, Leeds Metropolitan University

Chapter 1
A Coaching and Mentoring Approach

Learning to Leap starts from the position that everyone has the potential to offer more.

Having someone genuinely believing in you is one of **the** biggest motivators a person can experience. You can count on me being your one of your biggest supporters throughout the development process in this book.

Learning to Leap takes a coaching and mentoring approach to support you in your learning.

- What does coaching mean?
- Where is it similar to and different from mentoring, training and other disciplines?
- What have they got in common and where do they overlap?

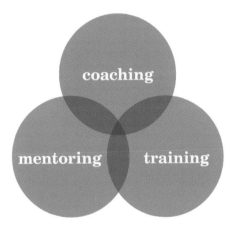

People often think of sports when they first hear the word coaching. Imagine you are a talented tennis player with great potential. A tennis coach will show you how to hit the ball over the net in a certain way and tell you how you are doing, but it's you that puts the practice in and plays the shot. Traditionally, a sports coach tells or shows you how to do something, apply a technique or demonstrate a skill. That's what the business world now labels **training or instruction**.

Sometimes we learn best from someone who has been there, done it and got the T-shirt. A tennis player may need someone beyond the narrow area of improving technique or physical conditioning, someone with a wider, longer-term perspective, for advice on match strategy, the game plan or long-term career. They are likely to have been an experienced tennis player in the past, someone who knows the pitfalls and has credibility in the player's eyes.

When you don't know what you don't know, they give you the benefit of their experience and open your eyes to new possibilities or ways forward. They can say what has worked or not worked for them because they have been in that situation, job or role. Like coaching, it's still your decision what choices you make. Business tends to call that **mentoring**.

The seeds of what business now calls **coaching** can be found in *The Inner Game of Tennis*, an influential book by US tennis player Tim Gallwey. He found that players performed better when they focused on psychological aspects ('the Inner Game') as well as learning how to hit a ball over a net ('the Outer Game'). The 'Opponent Inside' could be more challenging than the other player – 'I can't beat him', 'I'll never be as good as her', 'It's too difficult'. You may be a great stroke player when practising ('Skills') but crumble under the pressure of a competitive match ('Unfulfilled Potential'). So being self-aware ('Getting in the Zone') and knowing where you want to get to ('Goals') were hugely important.

That's one of the things that the business world has learned from sport. Gallwey suggested that fear and self-limiting beliefs 'interfered' and that coaching would help reduce the interference, enabling potential to be realised. He reduced his core concept to an equation:

$$\textbf{Performance = Potential – Interference}$$

Coaching in the business world has increasingly emphasised getting the best out of someone so they can get from where they are now to where they want to be. It's not about fixing people or telling them what to do. At its core is the unconditional belief that the answer lies within each of us. The coach's job is to help release that potential.

At its best, coaching is a trusting relationship between someone whose primary focus is to support you in recognising what you are capable of achieving. The role of the coach is in asking the right questions, listening so they can hold up a mirror to your progress and walking alongside ready to catch you if you fall as you work through what is right for you. Both coaches and mentors will provide support and challenge.

You may be someone who says you don't know what you want, who lacks confidence to make changes in your life and who settles for what you have – sometimes because it's the devil you know, and sometimes because you don't know what steps to take or what direction to head in, or you can't see the wood for the trees.

Learning to Leap takes a coaching approach to employability at some points and a mentoring one at others. In coaching mode, it creates the conditions for you to see more clearly, improve self-confidence, build self-reliance, and take ownership and responsibility for taking action to progress towards your goals. In mentoring mode, it feeds in experiences of my many years working and developing people in a range of organisations to enlighten and stimulate your thinking and action.

We will focus on your strengths as a starting point (are you making the most of them?) rather than on what you're not good at (which can sometimes make us feel inadequate). Yes, if there is a big weakness or 'interference' and it's getting in the way, we can't ignore it. This is where development and training can help.

Too often, though, looking first at what we can't do stops us from going any further at all.

A positive focus on the future rather than the past, on solutions rather than problems, on taking action rather than procrastinating, will ensure that you take ownership of the process. It can be life-changing.

And that's only half the story. You also have to practise, practise and practise again to maximise your natural abilities and to make it stick. This is what the author of *The Talent Code*, Daniel Coyle, has identified as the missing element of Tim Gallwey's equation. We will talk about luck or chance and learn lessons on probability from the world of statistics, but more of that later.

Later in the book, I reveal the paradigm shift we all need to make in our approach to learning and how you can seize an exciting opportunity to sustain your learning as you go into the future, whatever your circumstances.

Here's a handy way to remember the approach this guide will be taking, using LEAP as an acronym:

L is for **LISTEN** – learning to listen to yourself and others
E is for **EXPLORE** – the different ways to be at your best
A is for **ACT** – to achieve the best results for you
P is for **PERFORM** – making it stick.

Chapter 2
The Changing World of Work

How will the economic crisis change me?

It's become a cliché that change is happening so fast in the world that most of us are finding it difficult to keep up. Clichés exist for a reason and it's why jokes are enduring – there's an element of truth that underpins many of them. In some subjects, what students study in their first year at university can be out of date by the time they graduate; it is a fact of life today that the speed of change is increasing.

So what's driving change in its broadest sense? The big ones are that:

- we're in an era of economic austerity
- there is now a global marketplace for business and jobs
- a major demographic shift is occurring, with an ageing population and several generations in the workplace, and
- there is exponential innovation in information technology in the digital revolution going on around us.

Each of the above provides a backdrop to and informs themes throughout the book. If you haven't seen them already, take a look on YouTube at some of the videos called 'Did You Know?' and 'Shift Happens' to see startling statistics on change.

Hile Rutledge, CEO and owner of OKA and co-author of *Generations: Bridging the Gap with Type*, suggests there are three critical components of culture and environment that work on all of us, especially during our late childhoods and early adulthoods:

- socio-economics (how hard/easy it is to get money and your first job)
- general world events and social mood, and
- technology (access to information and choices).

His experience of development work on generational relationships is that the mix of these three forces has a distinct impact on each of us and on our development, and they impact the generations quite differently.

> **Common sense is the collection of prejudices acquired by age eighteen**
>
> Albert Einstein

For example, research has shown increasing dissatisfaction with working life. In 2007, a study of the working population aged between 20 and 69 across Europe by business psychologists OPP reported *"overwhelmingly, people feel they have not yet found their niche, are in the wrong jobs and are not tapping into their potential"*.

> ### If I'd known more about myself in advance... then I would've done some things differently
>
> Respondent, OPP report

They wish they had invested in their self-awareness, using it to better effect when they were younger and so making better life and career choices.

Research reports by the Confederation for British Industry and the UK Commission for Employment and Skills point to a skills shortage in the UK. In particular, employers are concerned that not enough young people entering the labour market have the employability skills they expect and want.

You might be a young person seeking work experience, entering the job market or wanting to go on to higher education. You are increasingly being asked to demonstrate who you are as a person, what your people skills are and how your strengths have helped shape your achievements to date. Matching what is on paper with how you present yourself in the marketplace can make the difference between success and failure.

Leeds Education Business Partnership sponsored a project on employability skills called Mind the Gap, involving three Leeds schools and employers such as Harvey Nichols and British Gas. The research found that *"the skills gap perceived by businesses is a result of young people often not recognising the skills they have and being unable to 'sell' themselves in a positive way at interview"*. The young people have developed a practical follow-up, Bridging the Gap.

The challenge is that business wants employable young people now. If young people can't manage themselves, how can they be expected to manage others? This book contributes to the closing of that gap, accelerating the process and engaging in the 'generation game' through a coaching and mentoring approach to build collective employability.

> ### Doing deals doesn't yield the deep rewards that comes from building up people
>
> Professor Clayton M. Christensen, Harvard Business School

So there you have some of the challenges of work today and tomorrow. Adviser to Barack Obama, Jim Wallis, asks *"How will the crisis change us?"* My question is how will it change you? You **can** choose to do things differently, to reset your values and to show employers you have what it takes today and tomorrow, irrespective of the availability of jobs at this time.

> **When we are no longer able to change a situation –
> we are challenged to change ourselves**
>
> Viktor Frankl, Holocaust survivor

What do employers want from employees?

> Being employable is more than having a set of technical and non-technical **skills** such as problem solving. It also includes personal **attributes**, such as having a positive attitude to work, and **knowledge**, such as understanding the needs of the customer and the business.

Employability is the jargon that is going to become increasingly familiar within Human Resource departments in the next few years. It's already a familiar term within secondary, further and higher education. It's the combination of the attributes, skills and knowledge that you need to have in order to ensure you have the capability to be effective today and tomorrow in the workplace (Confederation of British Industry).

It's no longer enough to be good at our 'subject' for us to be good at our job. That could apply to any of us at any stage of our working lives, depending on the context and situation.

There are three broad areas outside of your subject, field or technical expertise where you need to be effective:

▸ communication

▸ numeracy

▸ using technology.

This book focuses primarily on communicating effectively and how you can make your unique personality bubble to the surface and truly shine. We will make reference to using numeracy effectively and the role it plays in everyday life. We are also going to embrace relevant aspects of the Internet and social media as they increasingly play a crucial role in how we become more employable.

Opportunities

What makes me tick?	What makes others tick?
Opportunities	
Matching myself to an employer	Managing my relationships

(adapted from Daniel Goleman)

To begin with, imagine you are looking through a window with four panes. The view is unlike anybody else's – it is unique to you and presents opportunities.

Through the **what makes me tick** pane, see yourself for the first time as others might see you – your goals, motivations, values, beliefs, behaviours, desires, mindset, strengths, preferences and weaknesses. We will explore where these come from, how they have shaped you, what you already know about yourself, what surprises you on reflection, and what you might need to find out.

Now look through the **matching myself to an employer** pane, see how you make the best of yourself and what matches up with what an employer needs – your actions, behaviours, habits, quirks, emotions, moods, stress levels and use of time. We will explore what is working for you and what is not, and what to do more of or less of.

Look through the **what makes others tick** pane, see what other people are doing when they relate to you, how they are acting and behaving, and what is driving and motivating them. We will explore why they do what they do, how well you can read other people and their impact on you.

Now look through the **managing my relationships** pane, see what you are doing to make the most of your relationships with other people on a one-to-one basis and when working in a team – the attitudes, behaviours, knowledge and skills you need to do this effectively.

How do you feel right now as you look through your window? Is it clear, warm and energising? Or is it misty, cool and deflating? Is it a bit of both? Let's test the temperature on the other side of the window.

Creating my employability dashboard

Just like in a car, a dashboard will help you to navigate forwards. What speed are you doing? Do you need to slow down or speed up? Does the oil need changing for smoother running? Do you know what to do when a warning light flashes red or amber? The dashboard won't do the driving for you, but it will help you stay on track in pursuit of your goals or dreams.

You need to create your own dashboard so you can see how well you measure up against the core capabilities that employers want. Assess yourself against each of the following employability areas before you start. This will help you set a baseline against which you can measure your progress over time. The areas have been drawn from research by the Confederation of British Industry and The UK Commission for Employment and Skills.

 How **confident** and **competent** do you feel right now? Go with your gut instinct and score yourself on a scale of 1 (low) to 10 (high) for each area overall (the ones in bold) and then each element. If you are not in a job at the moment, think of meaningful past experiences. Maybe talk it through with a friend. Ignore the target columns for the moment.

Area	Confidence	Target	Competence	Target
Positive attitude				
A 'can do' approach				
A readiness to take part and contribute				
Openness to new ideas and constructive criticism				
A drive to make those ideas happen				
Self-management				
Willingness to take responsibility				
Self-starting				
Assertiveness				
Flexibility				
Resilience				

Area	Confidence	Target	Competence	Target
Work/life balance				
Time management				
Learning and personal development				
Personal presentation				

Team working

Respecting others				
Co-operating				
Awareness of interdependence on others				
Negotiating/persuading				
Contributing to discussions				

Communicating

Building rapport				
Listening				
Questioning				
Oral literacy				
Written work				
Networking				

Using the Internet and social media

Computer skills				
Understanding and using the Internet – especially search engines and social media				

Area	Confidence	Target	Competence	Target
Solving problems				
Analysing facts and situations				
Creative thinking for solutions				
Working collaboratively				
Numeracy				
Understanding the role and application of mathematical principles in the work environment				
Business and customer awareness				
Understanding the key drivers for business success				
Innovating				
Judging risks				
Understanding the need to build customer satisfaction and loyalty				
Contributing to the whole organisation				

We will return to this again soon, but for now let's stand back and look at these elements as a whole through your window.

What makes me tick?

▸ Positive attitude
▸ Strengths and preferences
▸ Weaknesses
▸ Values and beliefs
▸ Motivation
▸ Goals and ambitions

What makes others tick?

▸ Positive attitude
▸ Strengths and preferences
▸ Weaknesses
▸ Values and beliefs
▸ Motivation
▸ Business and customer awareness

My Employability Window

Matching myself to an employer

▸ Positive attitude
▸ Taking responsibility and self-starting
▸ Flexibility
▸ Resilience and work/life balance
▸ Assertiveness
▸ Time management
▸ Learning and personal development
▸ Personal presentation

Managing my relationships

▸ Positive attitude
▸ Working well in a team
▸ Communicating
▸ Solving problems
▸ Numeracy
▸ Goals and ambitions
▸ Business and customer awareness

Seem a bit daunting?

You may have heard the saying 'how do you eat an elephant?' and the answer, of course, is 'one bite at a time'. So that's what we're going to do. When you're faced by a huge task, feel overwhelmed and don't know where to start – think bite-size; what fits in your mouth and is digestible!

Go back to your dashboard assessment and rank the scores from the highest to the lowest. Start with the areas where you are strongest. It will give a positive boost to your confidence and remind you of what you are capable. You can then decide which of the lower scores to prioritise depending on your specific needs.

Now give yourself a target score against your scoring. The aim is not necessarily to achieve 10 across the board. Remember, even people with years of work experience will not be masters of the universe in every single area. You decide what to work on and at the pace that suits you. What would be relevant and realistic in your circumstance? Don't be afraid to revise your targets as you work your way through the book.

Chapter 3
What Makes Me Tick?

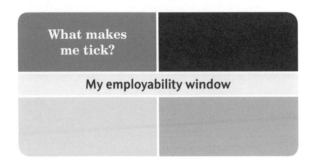

How well do I know myself?

What do I need to know about myself to help me be more employable?

Why is it important to spend time throughout my working life knowing and understanding how I like to think, what I feel and what I like to do?

How do I find out how I tick?

This chapter is part of the Getting it Right stage of learning to leap. It gives you a direct line of sight from where you are now to where you want to be through increased self-awareness. You are going to connect emotionally and intellectually with your personal vision for the future, your values, motivations and beliefs, and your various authentic selves. Without thorough reflection on what makes you tick, looking through the other window panes becomes that much harder.

Who am I?

> **We're all unique – just like everyone else**
>
> John Allen Paulos, Mathematician

Imagine you are standing on a hilltop on a beautiful, warm and cloudless day surrounded by a stunning landscape. Someone else is standing on a similar hilltop not far away. You can see them clearly and they can see you.

What they see is what you look like, how you present yourself and any movements you make, and vice versa. It's the stuff on the surface. What they cannot see is what you are good at, not so good at, what you prefer doing, what motivates you, your goals, ambitions, fears and dreams. And you cannot see these things in them.

How did you get to be that person on the hilltop? How did they? When you look down into the valley between you, why is that perspective unique to you?

Here are some examples of the kind of factors that shape us all:

- ▸ parents (or lack of one or both) and how you were brought up
- ▸ socio-economic situation
- ▸ opportunities
- ▸ close family members or significant others (eg teachers, friends)
- ▸ religion
- ▸ education
- ▸ health
- ▸ physical environment
- ▸ critical incidents (eg successes, recognition, failures, traumas)
- ▸ work experiences
- ▸ interests/pastimes
- ▸ personality
- ▸ personal values
- ▸ goals and ambitions.

Find a relaxing place to spend some time reflecting on your formative years; somewhere that is comfortable, familiar or inspiring to you. Identify the key moments in your life. List them and ask yourself how and why they have shaped the way you feel, think and behave.

- ▸ What have been the key moments in my life so far?
- ▸ What has influenced the way I tend to feel?
- ▸ What has influenced the way I tend to think?
- ▸ What lies behind the way I tend to act or behave?

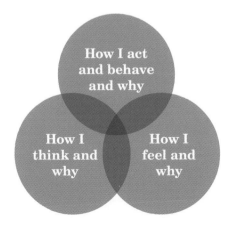

An enormous number of research studies and debates have been carried out on the extent to which human beings are the product of nature or nurture. Developments in neuroscience and understanding the implications of the brain's plasticity are beginning to further our understanding. Our genes certainly have an important part to play in who we are, and our life experiences then help shape our world view.

In the Wordsworth poem at the beginning of the book, *"My heart leaps up when I behold"* is saying that what we think as children, illustrated by his love of rainbows, determines how we think as adults. *"The child is father of the man"* means that just as a boy may inherit his father's characteristics, as we become adults we also have the potential to retain and develop the characteristics we showed as a child. There are echoes in the Jesuit motto *"Give me a child until he is seven and I will give you the man"*, which was the premise for the *Seven Up!* TV series following seven-year-olds through to adulthood.

Here's a true story about Tom and Steve to illustrate the importance of personality (with thanks to www.talentsmart.com).

In 1959 on an island off Japan, a woman gave birth to identical twin boys. The woman lived in extreme poverty, suffered from alcoholism and had been abandoned by the boys' father. It was too much to bear and she committed suicide soon after they were born.

At the time, there were many American soldiers stationed on the island. One of them, a sergeant, wanted to adopt both of them and return to the US to bring them up. It was against the regulations at the time to adopt two children, so he only adopted one of the boys whom he named Tom. Coincidently, the other twin was adopted by another US soldier, taken back to the US and named Steve.

Tom grew up in Kansas in a regular Christian household. In his teenage years he was keen on many sports, in particular, bodybuilding. It was in his nature to help people. After college and university, he set up his own business running a bodybuilding gym. He married a Caucasian woman and had two children, giving the first an American name and the second a Japanese name.

Steve grew up in New Jersey and was raised as a Buddhist, six states away from Tom. He too was good at sports, in particular, bodybuilding. He also liked helping people. Guess what? As an adult, he made his living running a bodybuilding gym. He married a Caucasian woman and had two children, giving the first an American name and the second a Japanese name.

Both men grew up knowing that they had an identical twin somewhere. In those days, the Internet did not exist! In 1999, forty years later, they finally traced each other and met up for the first time. Imagine the scene as they first looked at each other and saw their doubles reflected back as in a mirror. They even had the same gap in their front teeth. Once they got talking, other similarities emerged, such as the way they put their socks away in a drawer.

All a coincidence, you might say. Yet, this was the ultimate control group. What was the common factor? **They were born with the same personality.** The chances of this happening are billions to one, so this presented an amazing opportunity to look at why they ended up making so many similar choices in their lives. After all, each twin could have chosen a different sport, job, names for their children and so on.

The reason why they led very similar paths is that Tom and Steve followed their heart, played to their strengths and preferences and had been living fulfilling lives when they met. Researchers at TalentSmart in the US then tested this idea out on 500,000 people in 94 countries. They came to the same conclusion: that personality is a major factor in the choices we make in life.

So what does that mean for you?

You are more likely to be at your best when you know yourself well and consciously apply yourself to what you are good at and prefer doing more often than not. You can't play to your strengths if you don't know what they are.

Following your heart and discovering what really gets your juices flowing is more likely to lead to wise choices in career and life decisions. The result is often greater fulfilment in whatever you choose to do and being more comfortable in your own skin.

Still got some doubts? The BBC's *Child of our Time* 2010 Big Personality Test explored what the study of twins can tell us about personality. Nancy L. Segal, a world expert, found that

> Identical twins raised apart of course share no environments in common, but when it comes to personality they are as alike as identical twins raised together... what this is telling us is that the reason identical twins are so similar is not because of their shared environments but because of their shared genes [and] within the range of their different environments the twins are selectively seeking out or gravitating towards similar things in their environments.
>
> *(www.bbc.co.uk/labuk)*

How do I find out who I am?

Watch your thoughts; they become words
Watch your words; they become actions
Watch your actions; they become habits
Watch your habits; they become character
Watch your character; it becomes your destiny

Anon

Here are three ways to find out who you are as a person:

▶ reflecting on yourself, including the use of personality assessments
▶ asking other people what they observe and experience of you
▶ testing yourself through new and different experiences (then reflecting again).

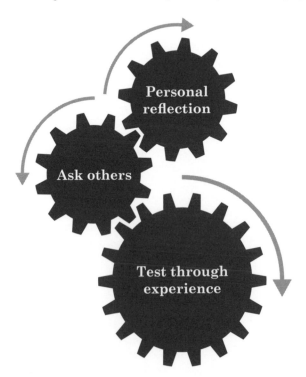

Reflecting on ourselves can be an uncomfortable experience. It's a skill we don't tend to spend much time on in our often hectic daily lives and it can seem indulgent or even embarrassing. However, it's absolutely essential!

Here is an exercise to get you thinking about yourself and to ease you in gently.

What do you know about yourself that is also generally known by people you know well? eg I'm very organised I play guitar I am a very quiet person I don't suffer fools gladly	**What would you like to know about yourself from other people who know you well?** eg When am I at my best/worst? What am I good at/not so good at? How do I come across in the way I behave at work/home?

How open or closed am I?

What do you know about yourself that generally other people don't know and that you keep to yourself? eg I do volunteering in my spare time I'm concerned about my lack of confidence I hate presenting in front of an audience	**What would you like to know about yourself that no-one knows yet?** eg I'd like to know how I'd respond under pressure or when I have a major setback I'd like to know how good I am at managing a large team

Want more support on how to reflect? Fast forward to Chapter 7 then rewind back here again.

What kind of personality am I?

In understanding who we are, it can sometimes feel like we have several different 'selves'. 'It depends...' I often hear people say. Why is that?

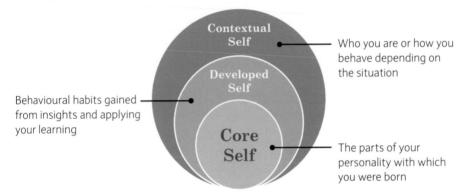

Remember our twins, Tom and Steve? Personality (**core self**) plays a big part in our life choices. That fundamental 'you' stays with you for life, although some areas can get emphasised to a greater or lesser degree over its course. Ask your Granny or Granddad how old they feel inside and, invariably, they will give a much younger age. It's because your basic personality remains fairly constant in adult life, even though your environment changes.

Our inborn tendencies develop as we experience the world and our characters get shaped by the environment (**contextual self**). We're all unique so we develop at different times and speeds.

We play up to or ignore aspects of our core self depending on our self-awareness or the choices we make (**developed self**). Although our core self may prefer to see the world in a particular way, we learn how to view things from other perspectives.

Many people have demonstrated the courage and will to remain true to themselves despite a harsh working environment (for example, whistleblowers). An even more extreme example is those concentration camp survivors from World War Two, like Viktor Frankl, whose spirit remained unbroken despite horrific conditions. Being true to oneself can be for good or evil, as any despot in history has amply shown. I'm talking here about acting for the good.

> Everyone has his own specific vocation or mission in life; everyone must carry out a concrete assignment that demands fulfilment. Therein he cannot be replaced, nor can his life be repeated, thus, everyone's task is as unique as his specific opportunity to implement it
>
> Viktor Frankl

Therefore, part of being employable means making the most of your various 'selves' – knowing your fundamental personality preferences, being adaptable and flexible to different situations, and developing the behaviours and skills needed for the workplace.

If you're struggling to identify your many selves, fear not, as help is at hand. You can use one of the many personality assessment tools on the market to get an indication of your personality and preferences. This is a way of speeding up and adding to the process of reflecting on who you are.

A health warning! No questionnaire will ever be 'the truth' as it can only ever be a starting point for exploring yourself. You are the final judge of who you are because you will always know yourself better than anyone else. Understanding yourself is the eternal audit.

> **Whoever undertakes to set himself up as a judge of Truth and Knowledge is shipwrecked by the laughter of the gods**
>
> Albert Einstein

However, as a starting point, many self-assessments are scarily accurate and can be completed online in minutes. There are a number of personality tools for you to explore, some of which are explained in detail in Appendix 2.

Whichever one you choose, look at your profile results and answer these questions for yourself:

‣ What aspects of my personality struck me as particularly accurate?

‣ What did it confirm for me?

‣ What aspects surprised me?

‣ Pick one preference from each of the areas of your personality profile and identify something you've done that demonstrates that preference.

‣ How can I use this to demonstrate that I'm the kind of person this employer wants?

‣ Write a paragraph on the kind of person you are:
  • pick out the most defining features of your personality, including something really positive about your personality (using the words or phrases from the profile if it helps)
  • link them to examples of how you have demonstrated this
  • relate them to what is wanted by the specific employers you have in mind

‣ Now revisit your paragraph and reduce it to a single sentence, one you could repeat with ease to someone else in an instant.

What job or career suits my personality?

The initial findings from the BBC's Big Personality Test experiment have some useful insights about your personality and the job you choose.

Dr Jason Rentfrow says:

> Those scoring high in Extroversion tend to be very satisfied in jobs involving lots of social contact, like sales, finance, law and teaching. This may be because those scoring high in Extroversion have a greater need for stimulation, which includes social stimulation.
>
> Those high in Openness were found to be happiest in jobs that involve creativity and abstract thinking, for example advertising, journalism, art, science, research and engineering.
>
> Those high in Agreeableness were shown to be most content in jobs that involve helping and educating other people, for example healthcare and education.
>
> Those who score high in Extroversion and Conscientiousness tend to like their job, irrespective of what it is. One explanation for this is that most jobs provide structure, which appeals to people high in Conscientiousness, and places for people to socialise, which appeals to people high in Extroversion.
>
> *www.bbc.co.uk/labuk/experiments/personality*

Brendan Burchell, senior lecturer with the University of Cambridge's Department of Sociology (and a contributor to *Child of Our Time*) says: *"people are drawn towards different occupations, they feel attracted to them dependent on their personality... employers are looking to recruit people with particular personality types for particular jobs".*

No employer would ever recruit you purely on your personality as you still have to demonstrate functional capability, subject knowledge or technical skills related to the job. However, in a competitive market where many people may have similar capabilities or experience, your personality can make the difference between getting the job you want or not.

> An employer is more likely to recruit you if you are a particular personality type and self-aware, than they would a similar type of person who is not self-aware.

Here are some questions for you to explore in your situation:

- ▸ What was I doing when I was happiest working?
- ▸ What do I like to do the most?
- ▸ What kind of people would I prefer to be with? What makes me say that?
- ▸ Who do I find it easy to get on with? What sort of people do I work best with? What makes me say that?
- ▸ What kind of environment brings out the best in me? What makes me say that?
- ▸ In light of the above, what kind of organisation do I want to spend my energy, talent and precious time in? What makes me say that?

If you take the Finding Potential personality questionnaire online, you will find a helpful supporting workbook for school leavers and graduates called *What's The Right Career For Me?*

Donna Dunning has written an excellent book called *What's Your Type of Career? Find Your Perfect Career Using Your Personality Type*. She uses the Myers-Briggs Type Indicator (MBTI) as the basis for her tips and advice so it helps if you have already completed it and know your personality code.

With the wonderful exception of Tom and Steve, no two people will have exactly the same personality. Now, there's a powerful opportunity for you to seize! Your unique combination of 'selves' is just waiting to be offered to the world and employers in particular. Getting the most out of them is your rewarding challenge.

Understanding your core self is an important aspect you need to explore to find the right 'fit' between you and a job. We will now turn to another major influence on your contextual and developed selves – your personal values.

What is really important to me?

> **The real act of discovery consists not in finding new lands but seeing with new eyes**
>
> Marcel Proust

There will be moments in your life when what is really important to you becomes crystal clear.

Take me as an example. Being a parent, bringing up children and being a humanist makes me think about what I believe in so I can instil in my children a set of guiding rules for being decent human beings and members of society.

Being self-employed, I have to consider what is important to me in doing business with people, how I want to be regarded and what they can expect from me.

Being a parent is about my personal life, being self-employed is about my working life. Personal values don't differentiate. They simply inform what we do whatever the context. A tension for many people is when work situations challenge our personal values. If they can't be reconciled, it might be a sign you are in the wrong environment for you.

My values guide my behaviour, like a moral compass. They are like a download lodged in my unconscious that gets played out through life. They help me decide whether to go in one direction or another, and help me make difficult choices or manage competing interests. They are also part of my identity. It often feels instinctive.

What has influenced me? My top two personal values are integrity and fairness. They come from my family background and how I was brought up. My parents were refugees from the Nazis in Eastern Europe in the 1930s. My father was a committed socialist and a criminal defence lawyer, then a judge, who had a passion for justice and standing up for the underdog.

This was a man who was at the liberation of Belsen concentration camp in his army days during World War Two. I studied law and sociology at university. I worked within the police service for many years.

In practice, my values manifest themselves in the way I do business and what I publish on my website so that potential clients can see the kind of person I am:

- respect for the client, partner or supplier
- encouraging respect for others
- openness, honesty and transparency in both supporting and challenging clients and in all business dealings
- genuine commitment and desire to make a difference to the lives of others
- going the extra mile when needed
- an underpinning professionalism reflected in attention to detail and reliability
- flexibility to changing circumstances and the needs of the client
- treating people as I find them at whatever level of an organisation
- embracing diversity in its broadest sense.

You can show employers the kind of person they will be employing by identifying and articulating your personal values and reflecting on concrete examples of how other people have experienced you demonstrating them.

For example, work colleagues give a clue to my values when they describe my attitude to work and how I behave: *"He cares about his work and professionalism. He is reliable and trustworthy. I know that if he says he will do something, it will be done. You can trust him not to let you down"*.

Someone who expresses what they stand for or believe in within a work context and tells people what they can expect from them and what they expect of others is showing leadership qualities to an employer.

Here is a scenario to test your values:

You work for a company in which you and your colleagues are shareholders. It has just been discovered that a colleague, who is also a close friend, lied on their CV about having a degree (a requirement) and said they went to the managing director's school when they did not. The person has been making above-average money for your company.

- Would you fire them or keep them? Give your reasons.
- What personal values underpin your decision?
- Where would you draw the line in creating your own CV?

What do you believe in? How have your personal values been formed?

Go back to the hilltops exercise as a reminder of what you have gleaned so far. The following exercise will also help you answer these questions for yourself:

Below is a list of commonly held values to get you thinking. Mark with a tick the ones that you agree with and with a cross those you don't. Ignore any that mean little to you or seem irrelevant. Add your own if they are missing. Check this out with a friend who knows you well and ask them what they believe your values are so you can compare with your own reflections. It will help reaffirm or challenge your thoughts and feelings.

Getting ahead		Looking out for yourself	
Honesty		Obeying the rules	
Contributing to the community		Having influence over others	
Maintaining physical appearance		Spending time with family	
Working hard		Knowing your heritage	
Loyalty		Building things	
Living healthily		Efficiency	
Freedom		Effectiveness	
Wealth		Creativity	
Owning material goods		Being religious	
Education		Meeting others' expectations of you	
Knowing the right people		Standing up for what you think is right	
Living in the right place		Keeping your emotions to yourself	
Achievement		Protecting others	
Competing and winning		Valuing difference	

Now rank the ticks in order, starting with '1' as your most important value, and do the same for the crosses.

Look at your top two values and, if possible, identify a situation where they might compete when making a decision. For example, if your top two values were 'wealth' and 'spending time with family', which one would really win out if put to the test by the role, job or career you are considering?

By really examining what you hold dear, it gives you a clue about what you want to drive towards or move away from in a role, job or career.

> ‣ What do(es) my top value(s) tell me about how I want to spend my life?
> ‣ What does my ideal work environment look, sound, feel and smell like?
> ‣ What kind of role, job or career would best fit my description?

If you know and understand your own values, you can also predict how you will respond in certain situations, such as at an interview or within a particular company or team culture.

When somebody infringes my dearly held values, they know about it instantly. There are certain words or phrases that trigger an emotional response from people depending on the values that are important to them. They are sometimes referred to as 'red flags' or 'hot buttons'. We tend to get passionate about the things that matter to us most. For me, it's when other people say 'you should/must/ought to do this...'

Test your hot buttons out by asking yourself:

> ‣ What would someone who knows me very well say of me?
> ‣ Think of a time when someone said something or expressed a view that instantly aroused strong passion in you, for example you got angry or upset.
> ‣ What did they say?
> ‣ What was it that got me annoyed?
> ‣ What effect did it have on me?
> ‣ How did I respond?

A really common interview question can be 'tell us how others describe you' or 'what do other people say about your key strengths?', or similar. These questions are tricky when you have only rehearsed what you think about yourself and can throw you when you are asked what others think of you.

So, our personal values can help guide our direction. In the business world, organisations also have values so you know what they believe in, forming the guiding principles that help them achieve their business goals, the behaviours they expect of all employees, and one means of promoting their image or brand. A lot to live up to and they don't always succeed!

Sometimes these are explicit and sometimes you only get to know the 'real' ones once you have some contact or experience with them. Here are a couple of examples of published values:

Leeds City Council	Tesco
▸ looking after Leeds ▸ putting customers first ▸ treating people fairly ▸ valuing colleagues. (www.leeds.gov.uk)	▸ understand customers ▸ be first to meet their needs ▸ act responsibly for our communities ▸ work as a team ▸ trust and respect each other ▸ listen, support and say thank you ▸ share knowledge and experience. ...so we can enjoy our work. (www.tesco.com)

Why is this relevant to being more employable?

You need to know, understand and make sense of the values of your existing or prospective employer for two reasons:

▸ In order to demonstrate how your attitude, behaviour and experience matches what they value, and

▸ In order to help you decide whether this is the kind of employer and work environment that matches your personal values and enables you to be at your best.

Find out what the 'official' values are of the employer for whom you are already working, or considering doing so. They can usually be found on the company website. Then ask yourself the following questions:

▸ What is my experience of this employer (eg as a customer or employee, from what I've read or seen or other people's knowledge or experience)?

▸ How well do they live up to what they say about themselves?

▸ How good is the match between my personal values and the employer? Does it feel right or not? What makes me say that?

▸ What concrete examples can I give of how I have demonstrated each of their values in what I've achieved so far in my life?

If you feel uncomfortable about the company culture or what the organisation stands for, this may be the wrong role, job, environment or organisation for you.

Aligning your personal values with those of your chosen employer will give both parties confidence of a 'good fit'. For some employers, this is as important as qualifications and technical or specialist capabilities.

What motivates me?

Knowing what motivates you is important to being more employable because:

▸ you are more likely to be motivated in an environment which matches your personal values

▸ you are more likely to be motivated by what you prefer doing, feel passionate about or are good at

▸ once you understand what motivates you, it is easier to identify specific examples of how it has impacted positively on your past performance. This gives employers a clue as to your attitude and character and how to get the best out of you

▸ questions often asked at an interview are: 'What motivates or demotivates you?' 'When are you at your best?' or 'What do you struggle with?'.

You are at an interview for a role or job and they ask, 'What makes you get up in the morning?' What will you say?

Other questions often asked at interview include 'How do you motivate others?' 'How will you motivate this team?', 'What has worked for you/with others in the past?' and 'Give an example of how you have recovered from a setback (What happened? How did you feel? What did you do? What was the result?)'.

Motivation is about the energy and commitment you bring to doing something. It's internal and you do it because **you** want to. You find things *motivating* when that energy and commitment is released by the conditions or environment you're in. That's external and it influences your behaviour.

The writer and blogger, Dan Pink, has shown from research that when people are paid enough (in their eyes), then the work itself becomes the focus of their attention. People are more likely to do things willingly and off their own back (or to get themselves up in the morning) when they have:

Autonomy	Mastery	Purpose
▸ Give me space to work on my ideas	▸ I want to get better at stuff and I'll even do it in my own time	▸ I want to make a contribution because I believe in this

Here's an example from my work experience:

> Gary was a police constable in his home town on the outskirts of Manchester. He had walked the beat for 25 years and enjoyed his job. He never wanted to get promoted and was driven by serving the community he knew and loved.
>
> One night, he couldn't sleep. He had been wrestling with a work problem that had been troubling the neighbourhood area he patrolled regularly. The more he thought about it, the more an idea began to solidify in his mind and he resolved to discuss it with his boss the next day.
>
> The problem was a spate of low-level petty vandalism and anti-social behaviour that had been making life intolerable for the mainly elderly residents in a particular location. When he spoke to the local youths allegedly responsible, they complained of a lack of anywhere for them to go or activities available to them. Gary's proposed solution was a mobile 'pod', as a place for young people to hang out with organised activities run by a youth worker. This could be moved from 'hotspot' to 'hotspot' depending on the crime figures.
>
> His bosses liked the idea and encouraged him to research the feasibility, establish costs and then set up a pilot project. It was a great success, reported incidents went down and local youths seized the opportunity to develop activities for the pod they wanted to see, or else moved away.
>
> Word spread among other police divisions and soon the idea took off elsewhere. Gary was encouraged to present the success of the pod to the local council. With my help, he submitted a report for a national award run by the Home Office. His bosses supported him by giving time to go on a roadshow to talk about the scheme to other police forces. When it was all over, he went back to the job he loved, patrolling the streets of his home town community.

Gary reached up and made things happen by his own actions (autonomy), acting creatively on something he believed in (purpose), taking responsibility and being accountable. He was given the support and guidance to realise his potential. He was true to his values, motivations and preferences and discovered some hidden strengths, and did it with great skill (mastery).

Motivation is one of the ingredients essential to performance, so it is vital you make explicit what motivates you to an employer.

Consider these questions to help pinpoint what gets you going. Talk it through with a friend, coach or mentor.

▸ When am I at my best? What do I do when I am at my best? How do I behave? What mindset do I have?

▸ What is my natural disposition? Am I more of an optimist or a pessimist? How has that helped me?

▸ Think of an example when your top one or two personal values have acted as strong drivers towards successfully achieving something.

▸ When have I gone beyond what was expected of me? What was my primary motive (for me or for other people)? What did I gain from that experience? What would I do for free?

▸ When have I been given the opportunity to be self-directing? How did it feel? What did I achieve when given a free hand to work on something?

▸ What have I done or taken up off my own back to improve myself?

▸ What demotivates me? Think of specific examples from experience. How did it make me feel? What were the consequences? How did I cope?

▸ Identify specific words that describe the exact opposite of what being demotivated means to me.

▸ Think of an example and describe what conditions existed that supported me being at my best. Use the following list as a prompt. Which ones are the most important to me right now?

  • enough income to feed myself, have a roof over my head, buy the essentials
  • stability and security
  • belonging, acceptance, being part of a group, team spirit
  • recognition from others, reputation, prestige, appreciation
  • belief in my potential, investment in my growth, personal support
  • development and advancement opportunities
  • having responsibility, authority, power
  • able to participate, voice my views
  • culture of learning, discovery, creativity, possibility, empowerment, trust.

There is always an assessment tool out there to help you if you're struggling to identify what motivates you. Try the *Strength Deployment Inventory* (see Appendix 2).

What am I good at?

There is something about the British culture in particular that means we spend most of our lives endlessly examining our weaknesses and trying to fix them. Think of the cosmetic surgery industry or possibly your experience at school. There is this sense that we are constantly being judged by others.

What if we were more accepting? Where would we start? By looking at what *is* rather than what *isn't*, what *does* rather than what *doesn't*, what *can* rather than what *can't*. As authors Marcus Buckingham and Donald O. Clifton say, *"develop your expertise in what is **right** about you"*.

The more you focus on what you have shown that you are good at and have succeeded in, and that you or others have recognised as positive, the better the platform for achieving your goals or dreams.

One of the most common personal development needs in business is how to give feedback effectively. Most people I come across in organisations immediately associate feedback with telling someone what they are getting wrong or not doing well. Many people are more inhibited in giving positive comments, praise or recognition. This is often down to a combination of being unable to recognise a strength in someone and embarrassment.

Knowing your strengths helps you to demonstrate your abilities and potential to a prospective employer. We have already seen that if you prefer doing something, you are more likely to feel fulfilled if you gravitate towards it. If you also continually practise working on it, you are more likely to improve.

Unfortunately, life and work aren't always so obliging. It doesn't matter who you are: we all end up being asked to do things we don't enjoy or find uncomfortable. The strange thing is we can sometimes be rather good at these as well.

For example, I'm an introverted kind of guy who, given a choice, prefers analysis, thorough preparation and the written word to spontaneity, thinking on my feet and presenting to groups. When I was in my 20s, I went on a communication skills evening course in order to overcome my aversion to speaking in public. Fourteen weeks and many sessions of excruciating discomfort later, I got over my fears and inhibitions. I got used to it.

Throughout my career, I have practised hard at working with groups of all sizes, from half a dozen to over 100 people in a room. Although it's not my natural preference, slow, incremental changes and adjustments over years of practice mean I can do it, and pretty well most of the time.

The point I'm making here is: by all means focus on your strengths as your starting point, but don't dismiss other opportunities to explore all facets of your personality and your potential. Taking risks and being persistent in tackling a challenge through commitment and practice are some of the ways we really learn about ourselves. An employer will want to see if you have that positive attitude and are prepared to take yourself out of the proverbial 'comfort zone'.

The baseline for being good at something is what HR departments call a *competence or competency*. This is a mechanistic piece of jargon that fails to do justice to a person's potential, but is part of the world of work. It's usually assessed against the three areas below, within a framework that supports what the role entails. Let's take a non-work example – parapenting:

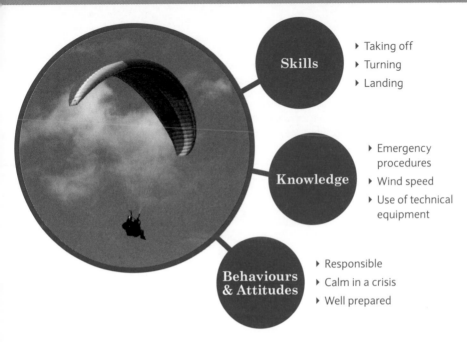

Skills	‣ Taking off ‣ Turning ‣ Landing
Knowledge	‣ Emergency procedures ‣ Wind speed ‣ Use of technical equipment
Behaviours & Attitudes	‣ Responsible ‣ Calm in a crisis ‣ Well prepared

Whatever role you see yourself in or applying for, it will be helpful to think through your answers to these questions:

‣ Looking back on my life so far, what are the things I have done that gave me the greatest satisfaction? What makes me say that?

‣ What are the subjects or information relevant to my aspirations that I know really well and can talk about or demonstrate with confidence?

‣ What are the skills I have shown when I have been successful in the past?

‣ What are the attitudes I brought with me when I've been at my best?

‣ Thinking of a situation when I was under extreme stress. How did I react? What did I do well? What does that experience tell me? Are there any helpful repeating patterns?

‣ Who do I know personally, or who have I observed in public life, that has succeeded in building their life intentionally around their strengths? What does that look like? What can I emulate?

Still unsure what you're good at? Have a look at Saville Consulting's Work-based Styles questionnaire (www.savilleconsulting.com), which helps identify where there is/is not alignment between what you enjoy and what you are good at (see Appendix 2).

Another way of looking at strengths is to analyse yourself in relation to the **power** at your fingertips. These are the personal powers you have going for you because of who you are, how you behave and what you've developed so far. Here are some common ones:

Positional	Expert	Reward	Charisma	Connection	Social
where you hold a formal position that opens doors for others or gives you decison-making power	where people come to you for your expertise or knowledge of a subject or issue	where you are a budget holder or are able to reward or recognise others	where you are attractive to others because of your charm	where you have an extensive and sought-after network of contacts	where your excellent interpersonal skills mark you out as influential and a key social hub

Put a tick against each one you have going for you. Check this out with someone who knows you well. Having two or three is likely. How do they match the need in the job or role you are seeking? How helpful would it be to develop an additional one?

Now look back at your responses in this section and the results of any online assessments. Imagine each room in your actual home holds your strengths. This is a robust home with strong foundations where you feel totally at ease. Go into each room, assign a strength or two for each and describe:

▶ what you can see, touch and hear in each room

▶ how that makes you feel

▶ what you notice that is different, if anything.

Periodically, or next time you doubt yourself, physically wander around your home and recapture what you see, touch and hear and how each room makes you feel.

What do I struggle with?

There is a great line at the end of one of my favourite films from the 1950s called *Some Like It Hot*. Cary Grant and Tony Curtis have been on the run from the Mafia for most of the film dressed as women in an all-female orchestra including Marilyn Monroe. They end up in a hotel full of retired millionaire widowers on the make for pretty girls. One such guy, Osgood, is infatuated with Jerry (Tony Curtis in drag). The unforgettable last line occurs after Jerry, trying his best to deter Osgood's advances, finally removes his wig and yells, "I'm a man!", prompting Osgood to reply: "Well, nobody's perfect".

I'm sure you have come across many people at work who would never admit to being less than perfect. They maintain a facade for all kinds of reasons including to maintain power over others, to demonstrate strength (in their eyes), or as a form of self-protection, particularly in a culture where development is seen as remedial or where second chances are rarely given.

The late Bryce Taylor, wise author and development consultant at Oasis (www.oasishumanrelations.org.uk), talks about the personal *myths* we create. You may recognise some of his examples. Add your own if you're feeling courageous.

I must always be in complete control of everything	Never letting anyone in on the secret that I am as unsure as they are about what is going on
It's the system that's the problem	Let's just moan about things together rather than do anything constructive
I am so compassionate because I identify so strongly with other people	I confuse your pain with my own and spend most of the time talking about how awful it was for me when I had the same complaint
It's my job to solve it all	If there's a problem, I have to solve it, even if the problem's yours and you don't want to solve it
People who matter to me must always love and approve everything I do	And if they don't I'll feel miserable and worthless and make sure they know it

This could get you down and I have known organisational cultures where this is the norm. To show weakness doesn't get you very far in these places. The very word 'weak' implies some notion of 'survival of the fittest', which is why other organisational cultures prefer phrases like 'areas for development' (although I accept this may test your level of tolerance for political correctness).

When you join an organisation, you will often find some internal systems and processes for appraising your performance. You may or may not find they are linked to development in your role and career path. In some businesses, you will be expected to arrive as the finished article, able to hit the ground running using the technical capabilities for which they recruited you. In other places, you might have been recruited more for your potential and put on a development programme or given a coach or mentor to accelerate the process.

In some places, the standards of performance and what is expected of you are clear. In others, they can be a bit fuzzy or completely absent. The emphasis in much of today's workplace is still on trying to eradicate the weaknesses, fill the holes in your capability and fix what is 'wrong'. Accountability in hierarchical organisations can lead to distorted behaviour if your boss's neck is on the line. It can be a negative, critical and sometimes judgemental starting point.

So, we could spend a lot of our time and energy on all the myriad things with which we struggle. We may eventually make some improvements, but many of us don't. Why is that?

Well, it can sometimes feel like trying to push a heavy rock up a mountain. Wouldn't it be easier and more natural to push it on the flat or down the hill?

None of us can be great at everything so it makes sense to invoke *the 80/20 rule* (The Pareto Principle, named after an early 20th-century Italian economist) or 'the law of the vital few'.

An example from the business world would be identifying which 20% of your customers account for 80% of your profits. Let's apply the principle to your personal strengths and challenges.

Go back to your employability dashboard and identify your 'vital few'. For each one, think through these questions:

▸ From experience and feedback, which 20% of my strengths have given me 80% of my success?

▸ Which 20% of skills, knowledge, attitudes or behaviours cause 80% of my challenges or blockages in becoming more employable?

▸ Looking back on my life so far, what are the things I have done that gave me the least satisfaction?

▸ What are the subjects or information relevant to my aspirations that I struggle to talk about or demonstrate with confidence?

▸ What are the skills I have struggled with when I have been unsuccessful in the past?

▸ What are the attitudes I brought with me when I was not at my best?

▸ Imagine a parrot on your shoulder whispering negative thoughts to you when you struggle with something (eg 'I'll never be able to do that', 'They are better than me'). Who does my parrot remind me of? In what situations do I notice this voice? What do I do to feed my parrot? Write these down whenever you hear them.

▸ How might someone who doesn't know me well see me at first?

▸ Thinking of a situation when I was under extreme stress. How did I react? What did I struggle with? What does that experience tell me? What unhelpful patterns keep on being repeated?

▸ Who do I know personally, or have observed in public life, that has overcome a weakness or vulnerability? What did they do? What can I emulate?

Remember your home full of strengths? Horror movies often have a cellar where the monster is chained! Facing up to our fears is one of the ways we grow as people.

Visualise your worst fears in terms of your skills, knowledge, attitudes or behaviours chained up in the cellar of your home (if you don't have a cellar, imagine one).

Go downstairs, take a torch and shine a light on the beast, look it in the eye and remember that you are in control. Remind yourself that the home is not going to fall down because it is built on the solid foundations of your strengths and attributes. How we overcome the significant things that hold us back is the focus of the next chapter.

Where do I want to go?

I've spent the best part of my life not knowing where I've been heading. For some, that's how life should be, a satisfying adventure with many unforeseen twists and turns. For me, there have been times where it felt immensely satisfying (when one door closed and another one opened, I landed somewhere with great people, stayed and made a difference) and hugely unsatisfactory (when I hit a ceiling or plateau, clashed with people or lost my motivation).

I have been made redundant three times in 30 years and been out of work for no more than a year in all that time. It is only in the last 10 years that I have gained the clarity, insight and maturity that come through life's experiences. Like the OPP research respondent, I am that person who wishes he knew then what he knows now about himself. So, goalless at half-time, I've found the net in the second half of my life. This book is about scoring at any time of the game to give you the best chance of winning.

Some people, like Tom and Steve, sense from a young age what they were born to do, such as helping others (in this case a gym, often it's a vocation like nursing and teaching) and for others it might be making money (running a business), or a combination of both. Many people have no idea where they want to go next year, never mind in five or ten years.

So why set goals? Clayton M. Christensen, Harvard professor and a business adviser to the CEO of Intel, has argued that the most useful learning anyone can do is to determine their life's purpose. Then all subsequent goals are a means of living your life's purpose. Your decisions about where you put your time, energy and talent will then shape your life's strategy.

What do you think about that? Is this your fundamental starting point or something to put on the back burner? What you want from work, a job or career will change over the course of your life. Where are you right now? These are questions we all return to again and again as we shape our destinies.

> **If they don't figure it out, they will just sail off without a rudder and get buffeted by the very rough seas of life. Clarity of purpose in life trumps activity-based costing, balanced scorecards, core competence...**
>
> Professor Clayton M. Christensen, Harvard Business School
> (on his students)

Let's explore the idea first and then you can decide whether or not goals help.

The idea of deliberately setting a goal for which you strive is common practice in sport and the corporate world, although the word 'goal' can put people off if it's seen as a bit of jargon. Give it your own label if it helps, but for convenience's sake I'm going to use 'goal'.

How you decide to reach your goal will vary considerably. Whether the goal is concrete, specific, hazy, generic, large or small will differ depending on your preferences and the nature of the goal itself. Ensuring you get up on time for tomorrow's interview, prepping for it, identifying your career direction and determining your life's purpose require differing forms of attention.

Some of us (like me) prefer to plan things out in great detail, with clear targets, deadlines and milestones. It is less stressful and I finish in good time. Others may set a rough goal and like to keep things open to allow unforeseen opportunities to emerge and be seized. They may change the route to their goal or the goal itself several times. Their creativity and energy increases as the goal comes into view.

What do you prefer?

Remember, opportunity and chance are important factors in finding the job or role you want, so closing down too early or not being flexible can be counterproductive. Changing jobs and directions is more common today than in the 'job for life' era.

Set your goal too high and it can become self-defeating and demotivating because it feels so out of reach. Set it too low and you can achieve success quite quickly, which is good for confidence and a way of tackling procrastination, but it may be limiting. It depends on what inspires you.

Beware becoming too fixated by 'goals' but, instead, see them as a series of guiding lights. In the last year, I've attended award ceremonies at a university and a secondary school where exceptional sportsmen have made the presentations. They have used their speeches to show that anything is possible even without qualifications if you want it enough (climbing Everest, running six back-to-back marathons, etc).

It is easy to dismiss these examples as being out of the reach of the majority of people. As the cliché goes, you can't win the lottery unless you buy a ticket. Even if you do, your chances are 14 million to one. But you could spend your pound on something else, so find a goal that suits your aspirations. If 'exceptional' means being unique, then becoming more employable is about recognising what is unique about you, acknowledging it, articulating it and using it as a means of exploring your potential.

A well-known acronym for goal-setting is **SMART.** It works best for short-term, task-focused goals and stands for:

> ▸ **Specific** – eg 'I want an up-to-date CV to send to recruitment agencies. It is focused, personal and forward-looking
>
> ▸ **Measurable** – up-to-date information on my CV, 20 agencies identified, by the end of January
>
> ▸ **Achievable (or Agreed)** – I know my other commitments and what's involved, I've prioritised my workload
>
> ▸ **Realistic (or Relevant)** – I've estimated how long it will take me and when I can do it
>
> ▸ **Time-bound** – clear deadline, I understand the risks or consequences for me of failing to meet it.

According to Professor David Clutterbuck, who has written several excellent books on coaching and mentoring (www.clutterbuckassociates.co.uk), *"for bigger, more meaningful goals, SMART fixates upon a single path, losing sight of other opportunities to achieve the goal. It's actually associated with FAILURE to achieve such goals. Much more important is linking goals to personal values – and to each other. When goals form part of a broader sense of personal purpose, they reinforce each other"*.

Carol Wilson, Head of Accreditation at the Association for Coaching, argues that SMART is more suited to situations when managers set goals for other people who are not involved in the goal-setting process themselves. She suggests an alternative called **EXACT** for setting your own goals based on a coaching approach:

- **EX**citing – positively framed and inspiring
- **Assessable** – measurable and specific
- **Challenging** – stretching and ambitious
- **Time-framed** – within a recognised deadline.

Revisit your personal values and then apply the EXACT approach to help identify where you are going.

- Specifically, what do I want to move towards (rather than away from)?
- How will I know if I have succeeded?
- What challenge have I succeeded in tackling in the past? How did it feel? What will stretch me further that I know I will enjoy even though it will be difficult?
- When will I have achieved my goal?

It is not always easy to identify our real challenges and goals. Canadian entrepreneur and Executive Coach, Andrea J Lee (www.andreajlee.com), suggests that you surround yourself with people who have big visions – *"You become most like the five people you spend the most time with. Choose wisely"*. Talk to people about what you want to be and do. You will suddenly find yourself more accountable subconsciously because you don't want to let them or yourself down. It will give you the impetus to take action.

The mental 'baggage' we carry around with us can prevent clear thinking. One way to uncover your real challenge is by using Nancy Kline's 'Incisive Questions™' technique. Here's an example you can adapt for yourself:

Imagine an 'older' person with typical assumptions about their employability:

▸ *What are you assuming that is stopping you from going forward?* That others think I am a slow learner, stuck in my ways, no longer ambitious, more cynical and less capable than younger people.

▸ *Do you **think** that assumption is true? Can you defend your assumption factually, logically or philosophically?* No.

▸ *If it isn't or you can't, what are **your** words for what is true and liberating instead?* From my lifetime's experience I have learned how to learn and deal with change, I know my strengths and how best to use them, I have different but equally motivating goals and I would make a brilliant mentor.

▸ *If you knew **that**, how would you go forward?* I would identify my goals in line with my personal values, draw on my experience of learning and change to create new opportunities for myself and other people, play to my strengths and contribute to the development of others.

A way in which you can positively frame your goal is to take leadership guru Stephen Covey's advice and *"begin with the end in mind"*. Focus on a positive outcome by artificially removing any barriers to achieving it. There is a psychological trick you can play with yourself that involves imagining achievements or success that helps neutralise negative thinking. It's a bit like rehearsing what you want. There are no problems to hold you back (lack of self-belief, the naysayers around you) because you have 'achieved' your goal. It helps to free your mind of the 'interferences' mentioned earlier.

It relates to the 'EXciting' goal of the EXACT model about moving towards something positive rather than avoiding something negative. Remember what it feels like to view a new car at the showroom or buy a new TV? We find that more motivating than thinking about what is wrong with our current one. Use this approach with anything you want to change.

Here is an example from my experience to illustrate the mindset involved:

I passed a part-time master's degree in management at Manchester Metropolitan University while working full-time in the police service. I recall the moment when I realised what I had achieved. I can hear the ripple of applause as my name was called to receive the certificate at the awards ceremony and being cited as The Chartered Management Institute's Student of the Year. I remember my feelings of satisfaction, elation, pleasure and relief. I remember also the letter of congratulation from the Deputy Chief Constable. That little voice in my head congratulating me, yelling how it had always known I could do it. I can see my wife and daughter outside the hall taking pictures of me in my gown. I can see the letters after my name in the programme. I feel good just thinking about it right now ('blimey, I did that').

I am also aware, looking back over my success, of the milestone events, the turning points and times when things seemed impossible (I developed shingles at one point and was off work for six weeks). Problems were overcome, and new things learned. Difficult people or relationships were changed, thus moving things towards my final outcome.

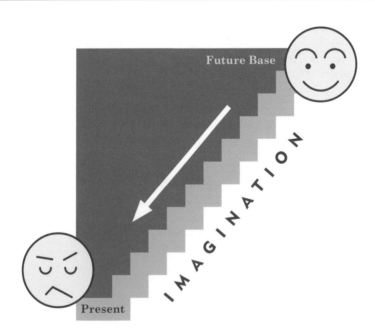

Mapping the future

There are four stages involved in taking Covey's advice and 'starting with the end in mind'. First, fix a specific date in the future when your vision has been achieved. The timeframe can be as short as a couple of hours, or several months or even years.

STAGE 1	**Build a compelling vision of your ideal outcome as if it has already been achieved (eg the job, role, career, success you want).**
	Identify some headings and write a sentence or two under each one. For personal and career development, typical headings may include income; job type; qualifications; location; time at home vs. time at work, etc. The headings or criteria are those that you would normally use to describe what **you** mean by success.
	If it helps, talk it through with a friend or group and describe your success in the **present tense**. In effect, you are behaving as if your success has already been achieved. Be as creative and challenging to yourself as you like!
	You may find this the most difficult part. It is easy to slip into saying 'I **will** be doing this', or 'that **will** have happened'. Maintain the discipline of saying 'I **am** doing this' or 'that **has** happened' for more effective results.
	Reflect your personal values and beliefs in describing success and use all of your senses to make it compelling:
	▸ What can I see, hear or touch?
	▸ What is my gut feeling?
	▸ What are the visual signs of success under each heading?
	▸ What evidence is there to be seen?
	▸ How do I and others talk about my success?
	▸ What does having achieved my goals sound like?
	▸ How does it feel, both physically and emotionally?
	▸ What **is** the sweet smell of success?
	When you are happy with your vision of success, come up with a few easy-to-remember words so you have a memory jogger when talking to others.

STAGE 2	**Work backwards to identify milestone dates and events, turning points and problems overcome on the way.**
	This is your 'critical path' to the success in Stage 1. It becomes your high level 'to do' list. Ensure it is chronological and matches the headings in Stage 1. Take account of known future events that may have an impact to ensure the process is realistic. Your priorities naturally fall out of the process.
	What must have happened for me to have successfully reached my ideal outcome?
	What happened 1 hour ago, 1 month ago etc?
STAGE 3	**Build in detail between those major events (eg new things learned, skills acquired, decisions made, people who helped me).**
	This becomes your more detailed 'to do' list. Ensure it is chronological and matches the headings in Stages 1 and 2.
	What did I do to make things happen?
STAGE 4	**Use the outputs of Stages 2 and 3 as an activities list, and apply forward planning processes to identify what resources you need and to decide what needs to be done in detail.**
	You are now in the present and planning forwards.
	▸ What do I need to make it happen (eg other people, resources, skills or knowledge)?
	▸ How will I provide these things?
	▸ What am I already doing which contributes now towards achieving my vision of success?
	See the route to your goal as a project. Look at stages 1 to 4 and create a real plan on a spreadsheet like the made-up example below:

	Month	Month	Month	Month	Month	Month
Milestone 1			▓			
Activity 1	▓					
Activity 2	▓					
Activity 3		▓				
Milestone 2				▓		
Activity 1		▓				
Activity 2			▓			
Activity 3						
Milestone 3						▓

STAGE 4 (cont.)	Life has a habit of throwing up unexpected developments, changes in your situation or new experiences as you implement your plan. Don't be afraid to review and revise it accordingly, including your success statement – ...*give it the freedom to evolve into something else that will bring even greater value* (Clutterbuck).

You have your ideal outcome (job, role or career), the roadmap to get you there and you know your first steps. Now the most important part – take the LEAP!

Knowing is not enough; we must apply.

Being willing is not enough; we must do

Leonardo da Vinci

If you struggle with taking action, leap forward to Chapter 7 for some support, then come back here again.

Finally, Brian Mayne has great online tools and processes for mapping any kind of goal at www.goalmappingonline.com. These are free and easy to use; give them a try if you learn better visually.

Chapter 4
Matching Myself to an Employer

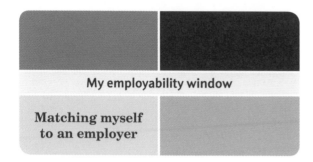

My employability window	
Matching myself to an employer	

> How do I show the best of me to the world?
>
> How do I match or tailor my best for what employers want?

The last chapter gave you a glimpse of yourself (who you are and what you are like). This chapter is about sharing who you are with employers in a way that demonstrates the skills, knowledge and attributes or behaviours that every employer is seeking (the 'how'). It's part of the *Doing it Well* stage. We will revisit the employability dashboard from Chapter 3 and explore the relevant key areas.

> To marry your own voice – what you're good at and what your conscience tells you to do – with the need of an organisation is a good match. This is a knowledge-worker-age concept
>
> Stephen Covey

Positive attitude

It doesn't matter what you have done in the past, what role or job you are seeking, what qualifications and technical skills you have or from which generation you come – having a positive attitude is an essential attribute that all employers will consider important. And it's all within your control, nobody else's. Every one of us can choose our attitude.

The challenge comes in adopting it more often than not, in the face of setbacks, other people's difficult behaviour and events beyond our control where there is often great uncertainty. The reassuring thing is, even if you struggle with maintaining a positive attitude, you can learn ways of getting yourself back on track – skilfully and authentically.

Why does it matter?

Being upbeat can help you and the people around you deal better with the pressures of a rapidly changing work environment. Playful banter (of the politically correct kind), fun and a lighter touch all play their part in creating a climate conducive to high performance. A happier workforce is likely to be more productive, better at overcoming setbacks and dealing with potential conflict.

What does having a positive attitude mean? What does it look like in the context of employability? If you are genuinely self-confident, your enthusiasm and positive approach will rub off on the people around you. This helps to create a healthy and productive working environment and encourages employee engagement. If people honestly believe in you and your capability, they will follow you.

Here is a true story of a student's recent application for a first job:

> Amy was in her final year of a university degree. It was November and she had applied for a two-year graduate trainee scheme with a well-known retailer starting the following September. She spotted the job advertised on Milkround.com and then completed the online application found on the employer's website. It required sending in a CV and answering some questions. She then completed, online, a numerical test (such as calculating profit margins) and a verbal reasoning test (such as the best and worst actions you could take in different scenarios that may occur in business).
>
> Amy received an email late on a Wednesday informing her she had been successful in completing the first stage but that all the assessment days were full (about 80 people) and asking if she would like to be on a reserve list. She was working on a university assignment that was due in on the Friday. Early on Thursday morning she replied saying she would like to be included.
>
> At lunchtime, Amy received a phone call from the employer asking if she could attend an assessment centre the next day as someone had dropped out. Her assignment was due in the next day and she had a part-time job commitment that evening. She arranged with her boss to find cover and spent the afternoon ringing everyone she knew but no one was available. Amy did not want to miss the opportunity so called the employer and said she would be there. If it meant working then driving up to the employer that night after work, she decided, she would do it.
>
> Amy continued to work on her assignment for the next few hours. Although not completely happy with it, she handed it in and drove straight to the nearest outlet of the retailer to do some research.
>
> Amy spent an hour and a half in the store making notes and answering the questions she had been asked. She took some photos but was stopped by security. The manager took her aside to ask her what she was doing! It took her ages to explain and she had no proof of the interview apart from an email on her phone.
>
> Amy drove home and started packing a bag. By this point her boss had said she could have the night off and he would try and find someone to cover. She had nothing to ▶

wear, so went out and bought some clothes she could not afford, borrowing some shoes from a friend.

Amy went back to the university library and spent the next two hours working on more research using an industry database and the employer's website. She also called a family friend who she knew had completed an internship in the company.

Armed with the data she had collated, Amy drove to a hotel the employer had provided where she settled in and then continued to go over her notes.

The all-day assessment centre was very intense. There were seven other people there and the day included five different tasks, teamwork and one-to-one interviews. Some of the skills on which they were tested included creativity, problem solving, teamwork and negotiation.

Talking to the other candidates during the day, Amy discovered they had all been invited to the assessment centre in October, so had had almost six weeks extra to prepare!

At this point, she presumed she had not got the job and started to relax because in her mind all she could do now was enjoy the day. She felt if she had turned down this opportunity, she would have kicked herself.

Amy was offered the job just before Christmas, one of only 12 out of 2300 applicants.

Here is a true story of a middle manager facing a threat to his existing job as a consequence of the austerity cuts:

Iain worked for a construction consultancy company in one of its northern offices. He had been employed as a project manager for three years, working on the building of new schools as part of a government initiative. There had been a consistent demand for the company's services in this area in the time he had been employed there. The recent change in government spending plans had abruptly reduced the demand and resulted in redundancies within the company.

Iain decided to act in his and the company's best interests before he no longer had any say in the matter. His wider goal was to become an associate of the company within a year. Recent feedback from a 360-degree review identified a need for Iain to increase his networking and profile within the company.

He approached his boss, knowing he was busy, and offered to take on anything the boss wasn't able to do. Iain soon received a call to take the lead on a commission in London that had gone badly wrong. He went down to assess the situation. The person who had been leading the work was an associate of the company and more senior than Iain. He had failed to deliver the agreed outputs for the client and the project was running late.

The client had been on the point of sacking the company unless the associate was removed. Iain identified several problems including lack of key milestones, a failure to engage the delivery team, and a lack of clearly defined roles and expectations. ▶

He also decided the associate could not be fully removed because of his considerable knowledge.

When he arrived, Iain found the associate uncooperative and inclined to block his efforts, so he immediately sidelined him by giving him only basic tasks. He decided to sit down with him to get him on board and asked the associate to work with him for the good of the company. This had the desired effect as, after a few weeks, the associate apologised to Iain for his initial behaviour towards him.

To get the project back on track, Iain worked with a more senior partner, and a young graduate who had become disillusioned by events. He engaged with the graduate, listening to him in order to understand his problems and soon realised his true capability. Iain gave him responsibility that suited his strengths and the graduate rediscovered his motivation, becoming a valuable member of the team again.

Originally, the client had been told the work would be completed by the end of January. This was unacceptable to the client who demanded it two weeks sooner. Iain re-organised and resourced the work accordingly to ensure the client's needs were met.

Iain and the team successfully delivered what was required on 12 January.

He was promoted to associate in May, six months ahead of his target.

These are both examples of what the Confederation of British Industry (CBI) calls a 'can do' approach. The features include being proactive, enthusiastic and commited. In addition, both Amy and Iain demonstrated a readiness to take part, contribute and self-sacrifice, and an openness to new ideas and a drive to make those ideas happen. To do that requires self-awareness and then, most importantly, the deliberate matching of strengths and preferred styles to the employer's needs and situation.

The enthusiasm and commitment came from within them. Amy knew where she wanted to go and what she would enjoy (working in the same field as her degree for a prestigious organisation). Although not first choice for interview in a highly competitive recruitment process, her CV and application were strong enough to get her an interview when the opportunity arose (chance or luck).

Once she knew she had an interview, in the very short space of time available, she showed initiative and drive to make things happen (doing the research, presenting herself well), running on adrenalin! At the interview and the subsequent assessment centre, Amy was able to let her personality shine through, demonstrating a readiness to take part and contribute in her own style. Managing herself in a stressful environment enabled her to perform.

Iain loved his job and wanted to keep it. He anticipated a problem, saw an opportunity to advance towards his personal goal and found a solution that benefited both himself and the company. Although he would have preferred to continue in the same area of work, he was open to the idea of changing course and was proactive in making it happen. He skilfully overcame a relationship difficulty through being assertive and pragmatic. His enthusiasm, commitment and skills rubbed off on other people, increasing their motivation and effectiveness for the benefit of the customer.

Both Amy and Iain increased their employability, now and in the future, through choosing a positive attitude and demonstrating it skilfully and authentically.

> Think of an example where you showed a positive attitude to tackling a task or challenge:

- ▸ What was the context?
- ▸ What was the task or challenge?
- ▸ What was my approach?
- ▸ What was the impact on me, other people and the task?
- ▸ What links can I make between this example and what this employer wants or needs?
- ▸ What does it demonstrate about me?
- ▸ Consequently, what would be the benefits of my approach for this employer?

Some commonly asked questions at interviews that may be a test of your positivity include: 'Tell me about a time when you made a difference to (an issue/team/project etc)'; 'Tell us about a time when you overcame a challenge by being proactive' and 'What would you do if ...?'.

Some of the ways you can develop and maintain a positive attitude are explored in the rest of the book.

Taking responsibility

Many people work in environments that are predominantly hierarchical in structure and culture. Tasks are passed down or distributed from managers to the level below. Sometimes people reach up to take responsibility for a task. Their motivation may be to seek a new challenge for personal development or to take the load off busy colleagues.

Inherent in taking responsibility is how you choose to respond when responsibility is given to you, or your attitude to seeking it.

There is also a difference between being responsible and being accountable. The buck stops with the person giving you the task if they delegate it to you. You empower yourself when you have the confidence and competence to reach up to take responsibility for something and are prepared to be accountable for decisions. In the workplace, this will often be within clear boundaries set by your boss who may also provide you with the authority to act, information to which you might not have access and resources.

Here's a real example from personal experience:

> I went to buy a new mattress for a bed at IKEA. Having found the one I wanted, a sales assistant in the beds section looked it up on the computer and its availability was confirmed. I simply had to find the relevant aisle in the warehouse, take it away and pay for it. When I got to the right aisle, the mattress was not there.
>
> I explained the situation to a member of staff. He checked the computer again and apologised for the problem in a relaxed, reassuring manner. Without consulting anyone else, he then offered me a more expensive mattress instead which I accepted. When I asked him how he was able to do that, he explained that he had the authority to make decisions up to a specified amount and it was entirely up to him to decide how to handle this particular situation.

His primary motivation was to make me, the customer, happy, so he took responsibility for resolving the problem. He had the information and resources to make a decision. He also had the authority to make that decision within clear boundaries. He was accountable for the decision which he freely took.

Some of us thrive on being given responsibility, others shy away and leave it to others because they are fearful or unwilling to act. Taking responsibility is a mix of having a positive attitude, being assertive and being business and customer aware, as well as playing to your personal strengths and preferences.

Think of **MARIA** and she will remind you:

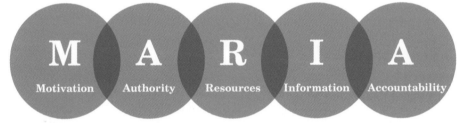

M	**A**	**R**	**I**	**A**
Motivation	Authority	Resources	Information	Accountability

 Think of an example when you took responsibility for a task or challenge:

- ▸ What was the context?
- ▸ What was the task or challenge?
- ▸ What was my approach?
- ▸ What was the impact on me, other people and the task?
- ▸ What links can I make between this example and what this employer wants or needs?
- ▸ What does it demonstrate about me?
- ▸ Consequently, what would be the benefits of my approach for this employer?

Self-starting

A self-starter is someone who is strongly motivated and shows initiative. Along with resilience, particularly in these difficult times, this attribute will be essential for getting or retaining a job.

According to psychologist Dr Philip Zimbardo, what motivates you at any given time is a complex mix of your situational factors, the system in which you operate and your personal disposition. We can only motivate ourselves – no one can do this for us. Other people can only create the conditions and environment that stimulate our choice. Leaders, managers or the people we choose to surround ourselves with have a critical role to play in this regard.

This is not always a function of hierarchy, as anyone's enthusiasm can fire us up when we are low. The organisations people work for can create systems that encourage positive behaviours towards the common purpose or goal. The harshness of the current external environment makes this doubly difficult as personal and business survival become priorities. I asked some of my clients what they thought people needed in order to remain motivated in these times of deficit:

- "Be upbeat and realistic"
- "Focus on a positive future"
- "Influence the things you can"
- "Have interesting work, responsibility, a sense of purpose and a good working environment"
- "Ask yourself, what's changed? What do I need to do differently? What do I continue or stop doing?"

Daniel Coyle, in his book *The Talent Code*, investigated what separates peak performers from the average, particularly in sports and music. He wanted to find out how their motivations differed and the secret to getting really good at something. He concluded that *"talent isn't born, it's grown"*.

He makes links with neurology and has argued that when we practise a skill to great depth (10,000 hours), we are upgrading the wiring of our brains and it unlocks talents we never knew we had. For most of us, this is probably unrealistic (10,000 hours is three hours a day for 10 years!). For a few, the right coaching, commitment and desire, added to this level of *"deep practice"*, has proven to be a highly successful path.

What anyone can take from Coyle's work is that the right kind of practice does make perfect and moving forward is achievable through conscious, incremental steps. Being a self-starter is necessary to make that happen.

> - What works for me? How will I motivate myself or remain motivated during these harsh economic conditions?
> - When have I demonstrated initiative that I can use to illustrate how I am **the** right person for this employer?

Here are some tips on self-motivation:

Remind yourself of the compelling and inspirational goal you deeply want to achieve	Find an opportunity to demonstrate or give a talk on something you are good at
Consider the benefits to you of achieving your goal	Show how you have helped others
Mentor someone or be mentored	Get organised, make a plan
Network with others	Observe or read about someone inspirational
Study or qualify in something you enjoy	Lead by example
Seek unconditional praise and recognition from people you trust and respect	Build what you want to do differently into your daily routine
Learn from what you have done well, take forward the best of the past	

Canadian coach and stand-up comedian, Shelle Rose Charvet (a consultant with a sense of humour!), is an expert on behaviour change (www.successstrategies.com).

"Real behaviour change is possible when you have the strategies to start and maintain your motivation, when you can see what you want, have placed the new behaviour inside a ritual you already do, believe it's possible, value the new behaviour and think you are the sort of person who does that. No, wonder miracle cures don't last."

Try her helpful inventory of Motivation Triggers to help you change behaviour in order to become more employable:

▸ Away from: I do not want...
▸ Towards: What I want instead is...
▸ Negative Consequences: If I don't succeed, what will happen that I don't want?
▸ Positive Consequences: When I do succeed, what will happen that I want?
▸ I can see in my mind's eye an example of each of the above.
▸ I have put this new habit inside this ritual or process that I already do naturally.
▸ I am regularly accountable to... for completing my goal.
▸ I believe it is possible to do this because...
▸ I have already succeeded at something like this in my life when I...
▸ This is important to me because...
▸ The kind of person who does this is...
▸ I am that kind of person because...

Assertiveness

Interviews for a job or role can be stressful and you may be challenged deliberately to see how you react. In a more positive vein, you may be asked to demonstrate how you have handled difficult behaviour or situations in the past or how you would deal with a scenario relevant to the job you are seeking.

What does being assertive look like?

I find many people struggle with being assertive, partly because it is misunderstood and partly because it is usually needed in a difficult conversation or situation from which we tend to shy away. Assertiveness sits in a healthy position in the middle of a spectrum between being aggressive or pushy at one end and being passive or unassertive at the other.

Here's a simple definition:

> **Pursuing your goals <u>and</u> the goals of the other people in the situation**
>
> Pedler, Burgoyne and Boydell

Being passive means not standing up for what **you** want to achieve or believe in, or not selling yourself. Being aggressive means seeking to achieve your goal at the expense of the other person's goal.

Remind yourself of Iain's story, the middle manager in the construction consultancy company. He showed his assertiveness in two ways. First, he went to his boss and explained how he felt about his disappearing role, what he wanted to do about it and why that would help his career. At the same time, metaphorically, he stepped into his boss's shoes to see his perspective and put forward ways his boss and the company would also benefit.

Second, the more senior manager he was replacing understandably felt threatened by Iain's arrival and behaved aggressively towards him. Iain initiated a meeting to assert his position and to understand the senior manager's anxiety in order to achieve a way forward that was acceptable to both of them. Iain's goal was to get him on board and the goal of the associate was to recover some self-respect and dignity. The outcome was clarity about their respective roles and an understanding they didn't have to be friends but they could work together.

So, it should now be becoming clear that some of the other skills and attributes we have mentioned so far support being assertive – a positive attitude and taking responsibility. Also important are listening, questioning, expressing yourself clearly, resilience, consciously managing your emotions, problem solving and decision-making, all of which we will address later.

At the heart of assertiveness is a proper balance between the rights and responsibilities of you and the other person. You will recognise it in everyday life. Have you ever been in a shop and had a dispute about a transaction where you said "I know my rights"? Employers and employees both have rights and responsibilities which they assert through formal conditions of service, job descriptions and organisational values, but also in the unwritten rules of what is acceptable behaviour. Unions exist partly to help people whose rights have been violated.

Here's a summary of the definitions based on the work of Mike Pedler et al. Where do you tend to spend your energy?

Passive

▸ My rights are often violated
▸ I do not achieve my goals
▸ I can feel frustrated and unhappy
▸ I can be inhibited and withdrawn
▸ I can feel hurt, anxious
▸ I'm easily taken in
▸ I feel bad about my weaknesses
▸ I often allow others to choose for me
▸ I get taken advantage of

Assertive

▸ I often protect my rights
▸ I achieve my goals without hurting other people
▸ I feel good about myself
▸ I am comfortable expressing myself
▸ I can be quietly self-confident
▸ I try to find ways to achieve my goals and other people's goals
▸ I can be open-minded and questioning
▸ I don't let my weaknesses affect me
▸ I often choose for myself

Aggressive

▸ I often violate the rights of others
▸ I achieve my goals at the expense of others
▸ I can be defensive or belligerent
▸ I can be explosive, hostile or angry
▸ I am brashly confident, boastful
▸ I am not concerned about others and their goals
▸ I can be suspicious, cynical
▸ I can be unaware of my weaknesses
▸ I often intrude upon other people's choices
▸ I take advantage of others

How can you demonstrate your assertiveness skills to an employer?

▸ Discuss a situation with someone you trust where you have asserted your rights in a way that resulted in both your goal and the other person's goal being openly acknowledged and taken into account.
▸ What was my goal in that situation?
▸ What was the other person's goal?
▸ What emotions did I feel during the conversation?

> ▸ How did I handle my emotions?
> ▸ What did I observe about the behaviour of the other person?
> ▸ What worked for me in achieving my own and the other person's goal?
> ▸ What was the outcome?
> ▸ What could I have done differently?

What can prevent you from being assertive?

Assertiveness is underpinned by self-esteem which is about 'knowing who you are, feeling good about yourself and being valued by others for the things you want to be valued for' (http://uk.personalstrengths.com).

Healthy assertiveness can be inhibited by lack of confidence or low self-esteem where we hold back because of fear or we bring our negative feelings to the forefront of our interactions with others when we feel threatened ('fight or flight').

With a prospective employer, that might mean:

▸ being a rabbit in the headlights at an interview so you fail to do yourself justice

▸ overreacting to a question when under pressure or being defensive about a perceived criticism (think of the interview episode of The Apprentice where Sir Alan Sugar's business pals deliberately try to provoke the interviewee)

▸ being over-confident, which can be a sign of nerves or can be seen as arrogance. Remember, a weakness is often nothing more than an overplayed strength.

Being employable means getting the right balance between making the most of the real you and the specific needs of the employer. You can show that in the way you present yourself in person in seeking a job or role, for example:

▸ at an interview or assessment day

▸ in conversations to build relationships that may lead to opportunities (at networking meetings, on the telephone)

▸ with recruitment agencies.

In the workplace, being assertive is a key skill that employers want, particularly in the current climate, because the environment is often unclear or difficult. It helps to get things done in a way that builds people up rather than knocking them down or walking all over them.

It is sometimes easier to avoid dealing with things because of how it makes us or others feel or to let things get to us so that we act too aggressively. Remember the monster in your cellar?

Fear may come true that which one is afraid of.

Viktor Frankl

How can you tackle this?

> Try giving your beast a name, so that it becomes concrete and not an abstract set of fears.

Life coach, Cathy Dean (www.cathydeanlifecoach.com), writes a blog in which she holds a three-way conversation between her 'Self-Esteem' (how she values herself at that moment in time), her 'Ego' (what she really wants to do, given a free rein and total confidence) and the 'Universe' (the wise arbiter and knower of the ultimate truth). It's her way of acknowledging her fears and finding a way forward. Putting pen to paper or finger to key can help acknowledge and challenge your fears.

If that's not your thing, try the wonderful Jim Lawless (www.tamingtigers.com), whose philosophy is captured in his book called *Taming Tigers*. Jim was a corporate lawyer who, when speaking on motivation at a conference, was challenged by an audience member to put his money where his mouth was by learning to ride a horse from scratch and winning a professional horse race within one year. Jim had never ridden a horse before but he succeeded, gave up the law and has built a highly successful business around helping others overcome their fears (taming their tigers) and reach for their dreams. His 10 rules for taming your tigers come with plenty of advice.

> Here's a process you can use with an example to challenge an irrational or self-limiting belief (based on a process by Bryce Taylor):

- *My activating event:* A job/role you want is advertised. You read that 100 people are applying for each job in your (desired) sector or area of expertise.
- *My irrational belief:* I'll never get this job.
- *My underlying beliefs:* There are too many people who will be going for this job who are better than me; I've applied for so many jobs like this before, it's not worth it.
- *Predictable consequences that follow:* I'll walk away/won't apply/go through the motions/wish I hadn't seen it.
- *Challenges to my irrational beliefs:* Where is the evidence that I'm not good enough? Somebody has to be successful. It has been their loss so far. My unique offer is exactly what this employer is looking for, it's just that they don't know it yet. It's a self-fulfilling prophesy if I don't apply. I can take what I've learned from previous applications and make an even better case this time. I can learn from every experience. There will be more opportunities. Giving up is not an option. I owe it to myself.
- *Successful effect:* Renewed energy, positive intent, more relaxed approach, self-esteem intact.

What can you do to be more assertive?

Back to the principle enshrined in this book – building on your strengths and starting with what's going for you. Here are some suggestions:

Ask someone who knows you well what you should do more of or start doing	Keep a diary of any experiences where you have been assertive (use the earlier reflective questions as a template)
Practise and try out different approaches	Identify what works for you
Observe assertive people and develop your own style	Get a friend to observe you and give you feedback on what you do well and any adjustments to make you even better

Flexibility

When employers want people they employ to be flexible, it can mean several things:

▸ being prepared to adapt to new challenges or unexpected obstacles, changing circumstances and new information

▸ appropriate 'give and take' in terms of responsibilities and roles

▸ contributing over and above the terms of the job description on occasions when there is a critical business need.

What does it mean for you? Rate yourself against the behaviours on the next page (adapted from a public sector organisation's competences):

If you are skilled in flexibility, you will...

	Excelling	Achieving	Developing	Ineffective
▸ recover quickly from adversity or disappointment				
▸ seek others' viewpoints and be willing to change your own viewpoint				
▸ be willing to modify your own assumptions or frames of reference				
▸ display patience, understanding and humour when dealing with change				
▸ effectively manage simultaneous tasks and demands				
▸ have tolerance for ambiguity and uncertainty				
▸ view disruptions as the natural result of a changing world				
▸ set and re-negotiate priorities during change				
▸ create back-up and contingency plans				
▸ employ the 80% solution when appropriate				
▸ change direction when necessary				
▸ shift gears comfortably				
▸ decide and act without having the total picture				
▸ not have to finish things before moving on				

If you need further development in flexibility, you will...

	Often	Sometimes	Rarely
▸ not be comfortable with change or uncertainty			
▸ not do well on fuzzy problems with no clear solution or outcome			
▸ require more information before you feel secure			
▸ prefer things nailed down and sure			
▸ be less efficient and productive under ambiguity			
▸ have a strong need to finish everything			
▸ like to do things the same way time after time			

If you overuse flexibility, you will...

	Often	Sometimes	Rarely
▸ move to conclusions without enough data			
▸ fill in gaps by adding things that aren't there			
▸ frustrate others by not getting specific enough			
▸ undervalue orderly problem solving			
▸ reject precedent and history			
▸ err towards the new and risky at the expense of proven solutions			
▸ over-complicate things			

So what? Now translate that into what your potential or existing employer needs:

- ▸ What are the links I can make between my self-assessment and what this employer needs?
- ▸ Which relevant example can I use where I have demonstrated flexibility?
- ▸ Consequently, what would be the benefits of my flexibility for this employer?

Resilience

I cried because I had no shoes and then I saw a child with no feet

My daughters saw this quote in an art gallery in Ecuador where they had been doing voluntary work. It puts the notion of how people cope into perspective.

In these challenging times, what makes some of us more resilient than others and how can you develop resilience?

The value of being personally resilient is rising. As organisations restructure more frequently, respond more flexibly to external demands and 'do more with less', this has created pressures on human relationships in the workplace.

The manager's job involves a degree of emotional stress and strain, which arises as a natural consequence of working in situations involving authority, leadership, power, interpersonal conflict, meeting targets and deadlines, all within a framework of some uncertainty and ambiguity. The successful manager needs to be sufficiently resilient to cope with this

Mike Pedler et al, *A Manager's Guide to Self Development*

You may or may not be (or want to be) a manager, but resilience has a critical part to play in enabling anyone to deal with whatever is thrown at them and to remain emotionally and physically in control so that they can operate well under pressure.

As Pedler et al say, it's about regaining balance, maintaining a high level of quality, being proactive, being physically and emotionally healthy, learning from change and emerging stronger, monitoring energy levels and learning to slow down. It means that you feel the stress and are able to cope with it by maintaining self-control, but not so much that you become permanently disabled. It doesn't mean that you become thick-skinned and insensitive.

In defining the resilience of his football team (Crystal Palace) in responding to a defeat, manager Iain Dowie invented the phrase *bouncebackability* and that pretty much sums it up.

TalentSmart reported on research by University of Florida psychologist Tim Judge that showed people who take control over events in their lives, rather than allowing events to control them, are confident in their abilities and perform better in their jobs. When hard times strike, their anxiety fuels passion, drive and tenacity rather than self-pity, despair and fear.

The prescription of TalentSmart's Dr Travis Bradberry is *"to anticipate and prepare for change, to focus on your freedoms rather than your limitations* (from 'life is not fair' to 'what I can change') *and to rewrite your script* (from 'hard luck story' to 'perseverance story')".

Other research suggests that self-management, including resilience, appears to increase with age. A study of 6000 people revealed a big difference between Generation Y (born 1981–2000) and Baby Boomers (born 1945–1965) in the core skill of self-management. Self-management skills such as emotional resilience appear to increase with age.

> **Experience and maturity facilitate the mastery of one's emotions**
>
> Dr Travis Bradberry

This supports a key message from an Ashridge Management School study into Generation Y, which is that many of people's attitudes and behaviours are more a reflection of their age than their generation.

It may come from the 'school of hard knocks' perspective but there are implications, given the demographic shift we're now beginning to experience. Will Generation Y buckle under the strain and how can Baby Boomers help?

Here are some other tips for developing resilience:

Find out how resilient others see you as – do a 360-degree assessment	Maintain perspective, balance and focus to help you bounce back
Have a guiding awareness of your values and goals	Operate from hope of success rather than fear of failure – make you own luck
Build in reflection time and seek support – find a buddy, coach or mentor	See setbacks as a manageable circumstance rather than a personal flaw
Recognise that the event itself is often less important than your reaction to it	Be results-oriented, with a high drive to meet your objectives and standards
Interact with a variety of diverse people	Set challenging goals and take calculated risks
Monitor yourself, know which emotions you are feeling and why	Pursue information to reduce uncertainty and find ways to do better
Realise the links between your feelings and what you think, do and say	Understand the stages in the 'change curve' and know where you are on it
Recognise how your feelings affect your performance – pick your attitude	Reflect on experience – *"Resilience is something you realise you have **after** the fact"* (Diane L. Coutu)

Check out the Emotional Resilience Toolkit (Business in the Community, 2010) that provides practical guidance in promoting the resilience of individuals and teams in companies as part of an integrated health and well-being programme. It has six online modules you can take for free at www.managingemployeewellbeing.com/bitc.

Partly attribute and partly skill, being resilient is going to be critical for us all as we face up to major economic changes and their impact on our well-being both at work and at home. An Ecuadorian child may not have a choice about what happens to them, but we do have a choice in how we respond.

Work/life balance

Many employers are increasingly giving attention to the health and well-being of their employees. Well-being takes a holistic view of a person and encompasses their mental, physical, emotional and spiritual fitness. The phrase 'work/life balance' is a misnomer – there is only life and it includes work.

These days many of us face competing pressures, such as family and work, the cost of living, social mobility, the speed of technological change and information overload. How well we respond to these pressures can depend on how well we adapt to, and are satisfied with, our rapidly changing environment. If we don't adapt well, we often become stressed.

If we are not functioning properly, we become a potential risk and a cost to our employers and, as stress levels, depression and absence are on the rise in the workplace, litigation and industrial tribunals are now commonplace. The average cost to an employer of sickness absence is about £700 per employee, with variations depending on the sector (Chartered Institute of Personnel and Development (CIPD) 2009), and £9 billion in lost earnings for the UK economy from depression (Mental Health Foundation 2010).

When looking at potential employers, establish the extent to which they provide a healthy environment where all employees are supported to develop and utilise their skills and abilities to their full potential. Look at retention rates and any published staff surveys. When choosing a particular employer, consider how much support it gives to its employees, including health and welfare benefits. Also check if there is access to an occupational health service.

From a personal perspective, think about diet, exercise, stress-releasing therapies (such as yoga and meditation). Undertake a personal audit of the areas of your life that are important to you such as health, money, family, friends, education, spirituality etc. What are you happy with at the moment? What do you need to pay attention to? In what ways will this help you to achieve your goals?

> Imagine life as a game in which you are juggling some five balls in the air. You name them – work, family, health, friends and spirit, and you're keeping all of these in the air. You will soon understand that work is a rubber ball. If you drop it, it will bounce back. But the other four balls – family, health, friends and spirit are made of glass. If you drop one of these, they will be irrevocably scuffed, marked, nicked, damaged, or even shattered. They will never be the same. You must understand that and strive for balance in your life
>
> Brian Dyson (former CEO of Coca Cola)

Here are some common indicators that act as possible warning signs for your health and well-being, as well as prompting any questions you may have of an employer:

- ▸ being able to cope with the demands of the job
- ▸ having an adequate say over how work is done
- ▸ having adequate support from colleagues/bosses
- ▸ understanding your roles and responsibilities
- ▸ not being subjected to unacceptable behaviours
- ▸ being involved in any organisational changes.

> You can demonstrate to an employer your awareness of health and well-being by:

- ▸ showing how you maintain your own health and fitness and how you have supported the well-being of colleagues in the past
- ▸ knowing the warning signs
- ▸ understanding different personalities/work styles and their response to stress
- ▸ understanding what energises and motivates you and other people
- ▸ understanding that everyone has a duty to recognise work/life pressures and to help ameliorate the effects of them on themselves and others.

Time management

One of the biggest factors that affects our well-being is 'time management'. For me, it's another misleading label in common usage because this is really about how you manage yourself and other people in the time available. Time is not tangible, people are.

One of Stephen Covey's seven habits for effective people is *"put first things first"*. In other words, managing oneself is about organising and executing around priorities to achieve results. Focus on what is important to you and what urgently needs doing and manage the distractions. Just ensure that prioritising doesn't become *"an avoidance strategy"* which, according to journalist and self-help commentator, Oliver Burkeman, results in simply re-organising your 'to do' list.

Why is time management important to employers? They want to know you have personal and professional standards such as punctuality and respect for others in meeting deadlines. They want to know if you can handle lots of tasks at the same time (a link with resilience), that you will be productive in a way that delivers what is required, and when, by an internal or external customer. It's about you providing an excellent quality of service in whatever capacity.

In today's information age, the reality of our lives is of competing demands on our time and the potential to be easily diverted from our goals. Our ability to get things done and on time will depend upon a range of skills, knowledge, mindsets and behaviours. Different people have different values, preferences and approaches to how they view and deal with demands.

If you have taken the Myer-Briggs Type Inventory, you will have discovered that you either have a **preference** for 'Judging' or 'Perceiving' in how you like to live your life. If you start from a 'Judging' perspective, you are likely to prefer planning things, being systematic and starting tasks or projects early in order to get it done; you are an organised person. 'Perceiving' is a preference for variety, leaving things open in case things change and exploring new avenues along the way; you are a spontaneous person.

These preferences are equally valid: neither is right or wrong – they are simply different. They have implications for how you spend your time and manage yourself and other people. We can also learn how to step into the other preference because life demands it sometimes.

In terms of being employable, it is important to understand your preferences, how you like to do things and what you are good at. You can then describe to an employer your approach to 'time management'. Be aware that the person interviewing you or reading your application will have their own preferences. You are at the mercy of their own self-awareness and capacity to recognise or value difference in others.

Also be aware of those strengths that are sometimes overplayed. Here are some common ones. Which would you add of your own?

Attention to detail	Perfectionism
Systematic, planning	Lack of flexibility, too rigid
Communication	Too much talking
Thinking	Paralysis by analysis
Spontaneous	Easily distracted
Enthusiastic	Over-committed
Caring	Prioritise other people's needs over my own

Your **attitude** to time is another factor. Remember your values and experience will inform your attitude. Whether they are about efficiency, achievement, integrity or creativity, they will affect your approach to time management. Using values as a compass enables you to keep on track through focusing on your own and the organisation's goals.

Some people's frame of reference is the past ('I've done this before...', 'This has worked for me in the past...', 'I'm quite traditional...'). Other people focus on the present ('I am doing "X" right now', 'I need this now') or the future ('When can you get it to me?', 'How long will it take?'). The trick is to give attention to all three. If you are too past-focused, your mind will be on what has just happened. If you are too future-focused, you can get ahead of yourself. If you are too present-focused, you can miss lessons learned or be short-sighted.

There are numerous tools, techniques and approaches available to develop the **skills** of effective time management. In my experience, they tend to favour being systematic. I recommend a book called *Give Me Time* by The Mind Gym, which is based on research into what works and is best used as a resource to dip into to address your particular time management challenge.

We have already mentioned some techniques and approaches:

- eating the elephant – one bite at a time
- the 80/20 rule – focusing on the 20% of things making the most difference
- assertiveness – the ability to say 'no' or 'yes' to the right things
- resilience – juggling several balls at once, dealing with time pressures
- a positive attitude – dealing with setbacks
- taking responsibility – meeting deadlines
- self-starting – making things happen, proactively managing my time
- flexibility – adapting to changing circumstances.

Other common issues affecting how we spend our time include being digitally connected and face-to-face meetings. The challenge is often about reducing the load (Do now? Delegate to someone? Do it quicker? Defer? Delete, not go or do, say 'no'? Disconnect?).

What is your approach to time management?

Revisit your personality profile and ask yourself the following questions:

▸ How do my preferences affect how I manage my time?

▸ How do my preferences affect how I manage the impact of other people on my time?

▸ Revisit your values. How do my top few values affect how I manage myself and other people?

▸ Revisit your goals, ideal outcome or vision for the future. To what degree do I spend my time doing those things I value or that help me achieve my goals?

▸ Where do I tend to focus in my attitude to time – past, present or future? What makes me say that? What balance is right for me?

▸ What example do I have of how I have used a personal strength to manage my time in order to successfully achieve a goal?

▸ What strengths do I overplay that affect my ability to manage my time? What have I done to address this so far?

▸ Review your employability dashboard. Flag up examples of managing yourself well from your experience you can demonstrate to an employer.

▸ How well do I get the balance right between being connected with the online world and being present/in the moment with myself and other people?

▸ What am I going to: Continue doing? Do more of? Start doing? Stop doing? Do less of?

Learning and personal development

What kind of attitude and behaviours towards learning and personal development are employers looking for? What would it be useful to know? Why is understanding how to learn essential to sustaining employability? What are the skills in learning how to learn? How can you demonstrate to an employer your preferred learning style and a commitment to your own development?

Learning is the fundamental process by which people at work 'become more than they were' and acquire new behavioural capabilities

The Chartered Institute of Personnel and Development (CIPD)

Learning to learn is a neglected activity. At different life stages, we experience different types of learning by default such as school, further or higher education and the workplace. All the rest is 'on the job' and the stuff of everyday existence.

People tend to look at the reasons why something didn't go well and learn lessons (sometimes). It is less common for people to make sense of successes in order to identify patterns, build on or replicate them. Doing so helps you *"head in the direction of where you want to arrive every day"* (one of Jim Lawless's rules for taming your tigers).

You have been building a jigsaw puzzle of your skills, knowledge, attributes or behaviours that contribute to becoming more employable. Some of the pieces in the jigsaw will change shape throughout your life, so it's important to be able to recognise where and how you learned what works for you in order to maximise your ability now and fulfil your potential.

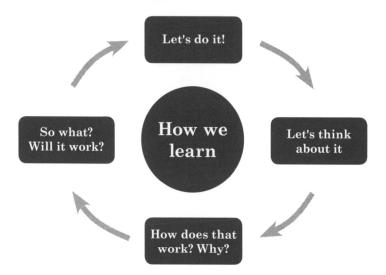

How we learn

The process by which we learn is based on inputs, decision-making and outputs. Sometimes we are thrown in at the deep end because work demands it or we choose to jump in. Other times we pause and reflect on experiences to see how it was done or to deliberately observe how other people do things. We also try to make sense of our experiences by taking them apart or making connections with previous experiences, then drawing conclusions based on what works or doesn't. Theories stay theories until tested out in the real world so we need to be concerned with practical application.

As we are all unique, shaped by our personalities and environment, we tend to have varying preferences for where we start in the cycle above, any of which are valid.

> ▸ Do you prefer to reflect first before doing?
> ▸ Do you prefer to be hands on first before thinking?
> ▸ Do you prefer to make sense of things first before doing?
> ▸ Do you prefer to see what works first before drawing conclusions?

You have already accumulated plenty of evidence about your work and life experiences; many of the suggestions in this book have encouraged you to reflect, then make sense of what works or doesn't for you. Testing out your insights and new ways of being and doing is the final action in order to fully learn.

You may be comfortable learning in a particular way through habit. The workplace demands that we are adaptable, flexible and self-starting. So it helps to develop a degree of comfort in different ways of learning.

Remember Shelle Rose Charvet's idea about breaking a habit? Place the new way of learning inside your existing ritual. For example, if you are not a great reader of business books, download them as an audio file and listen to them on a train journey. If your attention span is short and you value pragmatism, watch relevant short videos on YouTube containing 'How to...' tips. There is a Facebook app for MBTI Type Tips so you can have regular, short tips for your personality type automatically sent to you. Shadow someone you know for a day who works in the field on which you've set your sights. Volunteer to see what a particular job or role might be like. Take a risk and practise developing comfort in your less preferred learning styles.

For Jane Bozarth, an expert on social media for trainers, the common characteristic for what makes people learn successfully is the social, people and informal aspect. On a practical level, we might ask a colleague how to find some information or design a document, say, on a daily basis. Social media tools enable problems to be solved in real work settings. Tweet and ye shall find. We will return to this in Chapter 6.

Employers are looking for people who are rounded learners. For example, you may have had a range of experiences of job interviews in the past. Depending on how they went, they will influence how confident you feel about the next one. With interviews you can plan by doing research on the employer, the sector or industry and preparing what you want to say; you can also rehearse with a friend to test out your responses, but the actual experience of the interview will inevitably put you on the spot, require you to think on your feet and respond in the moment.

Irish philosopher and training consultant, Valerie Pierce, in her book *Quick Thinking on Your Feet*, talks about having *"staircase wit – the incredible ability to come up with all those devastating rejoinders just as you're going up the stairs to bed that night... when it's too late"*. Learning to think on your feet at the time you need to is about maintaining your train of thought and not getting thrown off track. It means being aware of false reasoning or other people's 'persuasive' logic at the time. Otherwise you can end up feeling manipulated and powerless to prevent it.

Pierce says there are four logical steps to becoming a clear and effective thinker:

- identify your purpose
- clarify your meaning
- think with passion not emotion
- change negative thinking into positive action.

So, if your purpose is to change your career or get promoted, *"the meaning you bring to it (and) how you think about it will determine your success. And how you get **others** to think about it will be the key to convincing them to come with you"*. Develop and practise the skills of *"weeding out the waffle"* – spotting manipulation when thinking on your feet. Pierce identifies 10 tricks of manipulation, how to spot them and what to do. A great resource!

Looking at your career or future direction emphasises the more reflective and investigative side of learning, so research skills are extremely useful. Networking requires all aspects of the learning cycle but you might start at different points, such as just giving it a go by attending an event or coming prepared to approach specific people with whom you want to make contact.

Whatever the circumstances, some of you will do all the above quite naturally whereas others will feel more comfortable about other aspects of the process.

Learning from success is about what works for you.
Revisit your employability dashboard and the strengths you identified:

- Where did I learn what employers need? (Eg listening skills as a volunteer for a confidential helpline, taking a specific responsibility at my last job, self-starting when fundraising for a charity.)
- How did I learn this? (Eg through experience of taking a wide range of calls, adjusting my style so I didn't interrupt too soon and trying out different ways of asking questions, observing my last boss who was very good at taking responsibility, on the job/trial and error as I'd never been a fundraiser before.)

Learning to learn is also about attitude. Expectations about learning and development have changed in recent years for both employers and employees. From my experience, in the public sector particularly, an 'entitlement' culture has been evident in the past wherein you joined an organisation and expected to be provided with training and development, irrespective of need. Now, the desired balance is that of the individual taking personal responsibility for their own development, facilitated by the organisation with a clearer link to business benefit.

Becoming more employable involves aligning your own development with your goals and ambitions while at the same time matching the needs of the employer with meeting their customers' or users' needs.

Your values and career direction will have a bearing on what you expect of an employer in terms of your development. Do they value learning or pay lip service? How supportive are they? Are they prepared to invest in you? How well do they listen to your needs and ambitions? What will you learn and develop with this job or role that takes you a step further towards your personal goals?

Organisations talk blithely about wanting a 'learning culture'. Very few achieve it. However, the aspiration exists in the more progressive ones so being aware of what it looks like can help you understand (or at least talk the language of) what employers are seeking. Adapted from the work of Bob Garratt, here are some of the features of a 'learning organisation' translated into what employers may want from you:

> ▸ **Future-oriented** – seeing beyond the day-to-day, giving attention to the future, thinking ahead so as not to repeat the mistakes of the past
> ▸ **Time to think** – debate about the future, reflecting on feedback and not just 'doing'
> ▸ **Questioning assumptions** – asking the right questions, challenge of accepted wisdom ('we've always done it like that'), being inquisitive or curious
> ▸ **Solution-focused** – putting forward ideas because you are best placed to see what needs changing if your job is on the front line dealing with customers or service users
> ▸ **Breadth of view** – looking outwards as well as inwards (to my colleagues, other teams, the wider organisational environment)
> ▸ **Balancing behaviours** – between task-focused behaviour and people-directed behaviour
> ▸ **Renewal** – reinventing yourself periodically (which means checking your goal is still the right one for you and adjusting it if necessary).

> Do you have what management researcher, Richard Pascale, describes as *"a relentless discomfort with the status quo"*?

The mindset is 'how can we do this better, faster, cheaper?' What hasn't this employer thought of yet? How can I contribute here, however small? It's about developing that kind of mental discipline so that you can help an employer stand out or differentiate itself from its competitors.

> ▸ What have I done in the past where I have learned through experience or developed an idea that has contributed to an improved way of doing things for the benefit of others?
> ▸ What ideas can I propose to a prospective or existing employer for their benefit or to solve a problem (without implying criticism of any efforts so far)?
> ▸ How can I learn in a way that suits my learning and personality preferences?
> ▸ How can I become more comfortable with my less preferred learning and personality preferences?

Here is a real-life example of a manager in the NHS who learned to explore the less well-developed aspects of her personality and less preferred ways of learning.

For the first time in her career of nearly 30 years, Clare was undertaking some personal development at a local university as part of a professional diploma. Until then, she had learned primarily from personal experience and 'on the job'. Her many managers over the years had rarely invested their time in her development so she relied on "common sense and what I do naturally" (the strengths of her personality) and what she had acquired as learned habits.

Clare is an outgoing person who tends to think out loud, jump into conversations, likes to know and understand the detail of an issue, and is hands-on and pragmatic, logical and systematic. When overplayed, some of these strengths become weaknesses and get her into trouble.

She is in an HR role that involves influencing other parts of the organisation. She found herself in a cross-functional meeting where she faced some resistance to complying with a specific process. In her mind, she knew what she needed the group to do ("it was obvious"), so she put forward her solution, dominated the proceedings and got her way.

Clare was being encouraged to reflect on her working style and approach as part of her course. She felt dissatisfied with the way the meeting had gone because of the muted reaction. As a result of an informal coaching conversation with a supportive colleague, she recognised that adapting her style to the situation and playing to other aspects of her personality would have paid greater dividends. Although these areas were not her natural way of doing things, she knew she could develop a degree of skill in them so she could get by if needed.

For example, by holding back at the meeting on her preferred solution, thinking before speaking, she could have kept things open (rather than closing them down) to allow ideas from other people to be explored and conclusions to be drawn through skilful listening and questioning, potentially leading to a different way of reaching the same goal but achieving greater ownership and buy-in to what was required.

A final word on learning: most of us grow up and continue to learn as individuals. Think of the classroom at school and how your learning was measured – coursework and exams. Think of how your learning is often measured and rewarded in the workplace – achievement of personal objectives and hitting targets.

In the future, there will be a greater emphasis on collaborative learning and working. Society is already ahead of institutions because of technological change. Learning how to learn collaboratively will give you a clear advantage in being and remaining employable. In Chapter 6, we will return to what you will need for collaborative working.

Personal presentation

In what ways do you present yourself in person to a prospective or existing employer? How do you present yourself in the workplace? In presenting yourself, what do you want to say about yourself? What helps and what hinders? Context is all.

Let's focus on any meeting or interview. Our impressions are formed through a combination of how much we trust and like someone and how much we think they're capable and respect them.

First impressions are important for the reasons we explored in the last chapter. Remember the notion of hilltops? Don't alienate people as soon as you walk through the door. Research by Dr Frank Bernieri, a Professor at the University of Toledo, found that people often make up their minds about how they feel about you in the first 30 seconds, or at least their unconscious preferences kick in. If they are negative ones, psychologically, you then have to get them back on side.

Recent research at Harvard Business School, supports the idea of 'fake it until you make it'. Facial expressions often give away how we feel and regular smiling is associated with changes in hormone levels. We can also sense when a smile is real or not. Now, a focus on postures has identified that holding your body in an expansive pose for as little as two minutes increases testosterone (the hormone linked to dominance) and reduces cortisol (the stress hormone). The result of this hormonal shift through practising this posture is an increase in feelings of power and a greater tolerance of risk.

> **For the most part people underestimate the powerful connection of warmth and overestimate the importance of competence... It's about understanding what moves people**
>
> Professor Amy Cuddy, Harvard Business School

A 'power posing' approach isn't for everyone. It can be helpful for people lacking self-esteem or with a sense of powerlessness. You may wish to explore further different ways to be physically expansive, such as using props like a whiteboard or flipchart.

As well as demonstrating your assertiveness through your body language – posture, handshake, the way you walk, tone of voice – how you dress can also affect perceptions. What would you wear to an interview, business or networking meeting? Are you dressing for you, for them or both?

When joining an organisation or prior to doing so, match the culture initially – what dress code is normal or typical for them – and do your research. If you feel strongly about what you wear (earrings, studs, clothes, hair etc), what will you 'die in a ditch for' because they are so important to you (a reflection of your values)? Is this the right environment for you? Where would you compromise and be pragmatic?

Expert image and personal branding coach, Katie Day, who runs workshops for businesswomen seeking to advance their career, says *"dressing with authority and presenting a professional image is about choosing an outfit that's appropriate to the environment you work in, while still retaining your individuality"* (from www.unlimitedpotential.co.uk).

You are more likely to give other people a favourable impression if you have a positive mindset that aligns with how you actually behave.

Self-confidence is being sure about your self-worth and capabilities. It differs from arrogance which is when your self-confidence is overplayed. What we think drives the way we feel and vice versa. In turn, both drive our actions. Therefore, your personal confidence can be built by greater self-awareness of your thinking styles and emotions, supported by skills practice. The more effective the behaviour, the better the result and the more this reinforces the new behaviour.

Here are some tips for developing your self-confidence adapted from Rob Yeung in his book on *Confidence*:

- show your self-assurance, create an impact, be present in the moment and develop your own personal 'brand' (What image would you like to project that reflects you and is one an employer will remember?)
- allow your personal values to guide you
- be a great listener, spend time focusing on the other person and ask open questions
- voice views that are unpopular and go out on a limb for what is right
- be decisive, make sound decisions despite uncertainties and pressures
- display assertive behaviour by stating your opinion, ideas, feelings and needs – clearly and directly – and listening with empathy
- hold in mind your strengths and how to deploy them
- be consistent
- be genuine and authentic – tell others about your successes and demonstrate humility when you get it wrong
- undertake an emotional 'cost/benefit' analysis
- keep a 'worry book' to learn new ways of dealing with anxiety-provoking situations
- hold in your mind what personal success looks like for your goals
- identify what is within your control and responsibility and what is not.

How you present yourself online is becoming increasingly important. Apart from the obvious vehicle of a CV or resume, putting a profile on a job site or professional networking forum requires a different and tailored 'voice'. In the same way you might check out the profile of a company with whom you are thinking of doing business, a company will want to check out your profile before approaching you.

You might want to satisfy yourself that the content on all your social profiles reflects you at your best. There are potential legal dangers relating to unfair dismissals and discrimination already appearing in the courts for throwaway comments said online in jest about a colleague.

Here are some tips for writing online profiles:

▸ focus on what value you bring to an employer
▸ demonstrate your credibility – what have you achieved? What evidence can you cite?
▸ match your profile to the medium – eg 140 characters for Twitter, longer for LinkedIn
▸ start with the why – Simon Sinek, in his book of the same name, calls the following the 'Golden Circle'. Open with what you believe in or stand for to demonstrate your individuality, followed by what you have achieved and then what you do (in that order).

The way in which you communicate verbally and in writing is explored in more detail in the next chapter.

Finally, if you are a student or recent graduate, take a look at www.venturenavigator.co.uk/skills. The University of Essex has developed a free 10-minute transferable skills assessment which has been extremely popular with students and university careers centres around the UK. You receive an instant picture of what your skills are and how they transfer to employment, with signposts to skills-related articles and training tips.

Alternatively, CareerPlayer.com has developed a bespoke psychometric test that takes personality and career value measures (www.careerplayer.com/psychometrics.aspx). They have asked everyone in their video interviews to complete the same test, and they then match the students to the people in their interviews.

So as well as getting the usual 'this is what you're like' and 'this is how you compare to the average', they also get 'here is a video of someone just like you'. It gets people thinking about careers they may have never thought about, but to which they could be very well suited.

More and more employers are now becoming interested in targeting students based on their character rather than the subject they studied or the university they went to. CareerPlayer.com say they are able to target their database based on their users' personalities and career values, bringing suitable students and employers closer together.

Chapter 5
What Makes Others Tick?

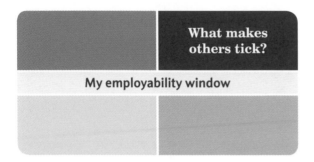

How well do I know other people?

What do I need to know about other people to help me be more employable?

Why is it important to spend time throughout my working life knowing and understanding how other people like to think, what they feel and what they like to do?

How do I find out how other people tick?

Many of the things we explored in Chapter 4 on what makes you tick can be mirrored in understanding other people. Your insights about yourself will make it easier for you to learn how to read others. This chapter helps you make those links and is part of the *Getting it Right* phase.

Positive attitude

Earlier, I talked about how anyone can choose their attitude. We can choose how we view other people in many different ways. How we choose to view people in a work environment can affect our and their behaviour both positively and negatively. You can begin to understand the nature of the attitudes others bring if you understand your own first.

Does this person have a positive attitude? What are the signs and how do I read them? In what ways can I tap into that to build my relationship with them? What drives their attitude?

Answering these questions is about getting to know someone. Bringing your own positive attitude helps to give other people permission, psychologically, to disclose. We warm to people we like or who are like us. Part of this is about finding common ground, often informed by our personal values. Employers tend to recruit people they like and who are like them.

Strengths

Why is it important to know what an employer is good at? Having some knowledge of current success stories and significant historical ones demonstrates to an employer you are interested in them and you are proactive. It will give you confidence to engage with an employer forearmed with some basic knowledge. Emphasising the strengths and positive aspects of the employer will immediately help to warm the relationship.

 Here are some initial questions to consider:

Employer	How or where can I find out?
What are this employer's strengths in their field or business area? What skills are they known for?	▸ Networking ▸ Online research especially the employer's website ▸ Industry/sector forums and journals ▸ Newspapers especially business sections (printed or online) ▸ People you know who work there/have worked there or other people you know who have these connections ▸ Recruitment agencies ▸ Internship/work placement
What do they do well/better/differently that gives them an advantage over their competitors or similar types of organisation?	As above plus ask someone who works for their competitors and ask their customers or users
What are their visible signs of success? What industry/sector awards have they won recently?	As above plus plaques on the wall in reception, client or customer testimonials, share prices, published performance indicators etc

At a personal level, you can ask yourself similar questions. How can I recognise someone else's strengths and preferences? What would it be useful to know so I can tap into this to build my relationship with them? How do they use their strengths and preferences?

Personal	How or where can I find out?
What are this person's strengths in their field or business area?	▶ Networking meeting or event ▶ Online research such as their LinkedIn profile and activity (forums they belong to, books they read, nature of their connections, questions they have asked)
What do I know about this person? What have they disclosed to me already? What else do I need to find out?	▶ Correspondence/telephone conversations ▶ Other people's information (treat carefully – they may be biased, gossip etc)
What are this person's interests, professional background/career? What do they tell me about their skills and track record?	▶ Ask them ▶ Ask someone who knows them well
What do I observe that this person does well? What skills, knowledge, attitudes or behaviours do they demonstrate?	▶ Behavioural cues in the moment ▶ The reactions of other people (but own your view)

Building a relationship with other people so you get to understand what makes them tick is going to happen best when meeting face-to-face. In an employability context, this is likely to be at a formal or informal meeting, event or interview. When you are in that situation, collect some real-time information about them during the interaction.

What kind of person are they? What do you notice about how this person thinks, feels and behaves? How is it like you? How is it different?

If people play to their personality type preferences, you can pick up on some behaviour cues that can indicate how they like to do things. Remember, behaviour is about choice so be aware that the other person may have learned a particular behaviour and it can mask their true preference. Test out your perceptions of their behaviour over time if you get the opportunity to see recurring patterns of behaviour. As a rough guide, look out for the following:

An outgoing person	loves talking, thinks aloud, interrupts
A reserved person	thinks things through before speaking, pauses to reflect
A pragmatic person	concerned with detail, concrete information/ facts, the here and now
An intuitive person	concerned with ideas, talking in general terms, possibilities
A logical person	objective, tests your thinking or knowledge, task-focused
A warm person	subjective, interested in what they or you value, person focused
An organised person	likes punctuality, systems, planning, decides early
A spontaneous person	likes being in the moment, keeps things open, decides last minute

How might the other person prefer to learn about you? How could you respond to match their preferred learning style? To be more:

▶ action-oriented?
▶ reflective?
▶ theoretical?
▶ pragmatic?

Here's a checklist for developing your antenna for other people's strengths and preferences:

▶ Am I consciously noticing my similarities and differences with other people?
▶ Am I playing to my strengths/trying new ways to understand how others tick?
▶ Am I discovering what works and what doesn't for me about reading other people?
▶ Am I seizing opportunities to practise rapport building with other people?
▶ Am I taking manageable risks/stretching myself?

Weaknesses

Understanding what other people struggle with provides you with insight into how you can support them or how you could step up if appropriate and contribute if they happen to be strengths for you. Employers that promote teamworking are looking for people with complementary skills.

Identifying an employer's weaknesses needs some careful thought. On the one hand, it can be a useful exercise in considering whether you want a job or role with them. On the other hand, if you decide to go ahead, take a positive approach during the recruitment process. This might mean not mentioning the weaknesses, reframing specific issues to show why they need you and how you can help address a problem. The ever-present danger of criticising can lurk nearby.

This book takes a solution-focused approach to being employable. That means focusing on positive ways forward rather than the negative pull of seeing nothing but problems. Identifying weaknesses can demonstrate your analytical abilities as long as your approach is underpinned by good intent (you will need to make this explicit) and supported by alternatives or options.

Values and beliefs

What is important to an employer? What drives another person? How can I recognise someone else's or an organisation's values and beliefs? What if they are very different from mine? How can understanding these support me in being more employable?

In Chapter 3, you explored the unique view from your hilltop and what has influenced it. With another individual, you can't physically see or touch their values and beliefs. The key is to build genuine rapport with them so that they open up and disclose information about themselves that will give you clues about what is important to them. The core skills are observing, listening and questioning, supported by non-verbal behaviours (see chapter 6).

With an organisation, you can see their values as they are likely to have published their ethos formally on a website or printed material. Testing out whether these values are lived within the organisation, or if alternative informal values and beliefs also exist, involves observing, listening and questioning.

Let's take an everyday scenario to test your assumptions of other people:

You are driving down the motorway at night with your friends or family at 70mph. The road is reasonably busy and you are keeping plenty of distance from the car in front. You decide to increase speed sufficiently in order to overtake. As you do so, a car comes up behind at great speed flashing their lights at you to move out of the way. You can see that it is not a police vehicle or ambulance, but a sports car.

What goes immediately through your mind?

You might take the view the driver behind is rude and possibly dangerous. Alternatively, you may think this person has an emergency and legitimately needs to get somewhere very quickly (for example, to get to a hospital).

What values are potentially at play here? It depends on what is important to you and them. For you, it may be a strong belief in being law-abiding, or safety conscious, or averse to risk-taking, or always giving someone the benefit of the doubt, or live and let live. For the other driver it may be any of those things and this is an exceptional circumstance, or belief in risk-taking, or a love of speed, or looking after themselves before others, and so on.

You can't tell and yet many of us rush to judgement or make ill-informed assumptions. Deliberately seeking to uncover assumptions is a good starting point to identify another person's values and beliefs. It relies on you being open-minded and flexible in your approach.

You may find that the person interviewing you for a job or role has a fixed view of the world. They may not welcome or recognise difference and prefer to recruit in their own image. This can be a choice and a challenge for you.

Do you want to work for this organisation or section? If you do, what is that person's world view? If it goes against your values and beliefs, are you prepared to look beyond this person? Test the water by asking questions about the issues that matter to you, for example, their attitude to flexible working.

The kind of questions to ask yourself in order to uncover another person's values, and where they might be different from your own, include:

▸ What is it about their words that resonates with you/upsets you?
▸ What is important to you about that?
▸ What would you have wanted them to say?
▸ What do you value in a relationship?
▸ What is important to them in this situation?
▸ What are they not saying?

I once went through an assessment centre and was at the end of a second interview for a consultancy role. It had all gone really well and I was keen to join if offered the job. The panel asked me if I had any questions for them. After asking 'what is the best thing about working for this company?' and getting a satisfactory answer, I then asked 'what is the worst thing about working for this company?' The response resulted in me turning the job down as it seriously challenged what was most important to me.

You will always meet people in the workplace whose personal values may not be the same as yours. You will still have to work alongside them or for them or manage them. The next chapter supports you with ways to manage those relationships healthily and productively. If the recruitment process is a good one, it should ensure a reasonably close match between those recruited and the values and beliefs of the employer.

Business and customer awareness

According to the CBI, employers expect people to have a basic understanding of the key drivers for business success – including the importance of innovation and taking calculated risks – and the need to build customer satisfaction and customer loyalty.

Innocent, the producers of smoothies, state on their website that they believe in keeping *"the main thing the main thing"*. In the private sector, the main thing for them is being *"a commercial business and so creating growth and profit for us and our customers is central to what we do and why we are here"*. (www.innocentdrinks.co.uk)

For St Gemma's Hospice, in the public sector, their purpose according to their website is to *"provide compassionate and skilled specialist palliative care of the highest quality, both in the Hospice and in the community"*. (www.st-gemma.co.uk)

Having the attributes described by the CBI enable you to understand where you fit into the organisation, connect you to its purpose and direction and help you with decision-making. In theory, it's about achieving a match between what you contribute, the needs of the business and the wants of the customer or service user. Making a meaningful difference is often cited as a motivating factor for employees.

In practice, you might find it difficult to see the clear link between what you do and the results of the business. It's clear if you are a nurse or doctor treating a patient or a sales assistant selling goods in a shop. It becomes less clear when you are part of a long supply chain and there are several links in between you and the customer or service user.

I once helped to design and facilitate an event for a whole division of an organisation with over 100 people in attendance. With the help of a design group drawn from the audience, we identified a highly successful project to demonstrate the value of different contributions to its success. We briefed half a dozen people to speak about their role and how it connected to the next person's contribution in the chain. It started with the travel clerk and how she had arranged the overseas travel for a large number of people, moved through various tasks that had to be achieved and ended with the head of the division explaining his role and the results for the business from the project. It was the first time some of the people in the chain had heard this.

What story could you tell to demonstrate your awareness of the business?

Staying aware involves keeping up to date and abreast of developments and changes in the business or organisation's environment. Employers are looking for people who are proactive so they can spot opportunities or respond to changes. A useful acronym for scanning developments in your industry or sector environment is **PESTLE**:

In practice, this can mean:

▸ staying up to date in the industry you work in through trade press, the internet, conferences, exhibitions and professional bodies

▸ maintaining your awareness of the economic environment as it impacts the behaviour of customers and other organisations by reading the business pages and watching the news

▸ subscribing to relevant blogs and online newsletters, joining forums and asking questions on LinkedIn

▸ developing relationships with other areas of the organisation through networking, as internal awareness is just as important as external awareness; regularly discuss issues with them affecting your area

▸ finding out how the organisation is perceived externally; read customer survey reports and industry commentators

▸ monitoring the performance of the business such as share price or other indicators for your department; be aware of how well the organisation is doing.

How can you identify what a customer wants or needs?

Try using a technique called the Customer Window. You can complete this for any person or group of people you want to satisfy. It's based on two questions:

▸ What does the customer *want* and *not want* from our service?
▸ What does the customer *get* and *not get* from our service?

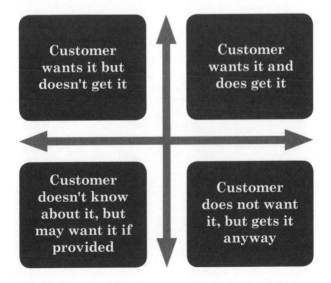

Customer wants it but doesn't get it

Customer wants it and does get it

Customer doesn't know about it, but may want it if provided

Customer does not want it, but gets it anyway

Customer loyalty is based on a wide range of factors including brand, price and quality. In employability terms, focus on what is within your control or sphere of influence. When you communicate and engage with customers or service users, you are representing the organisation and that may be their only contact. To the customer, you **are** the organisation and how you satisfy the customer reflects the quality of the service they experience.

Remember the story about the sales assistant in IKEA taking responsibility to make me a happy customer? I bought a better mattress, came away more satisfied than if I had bought the one I went for and the experience encouraged me to return. This is an example of what is sometimes called 'service recovery'.

Another approach to help achieve customer satisfaction is to identify and close the gaps in perception between a customer's expectations and requirements and their actual experience. This is about quality assurance and ensuring that both you and the customer have a common perception of what is required at each contact stage.

One aspect of internal customer awareness is being politically astute. Politics exist in every organisation. Research by Roffey Park found that what distinguishes destructive from constructive politics for most people is the intention or motive behind the behaviour.

Positive political behaviour is about acting with integrity in meeting both your agenda and the organisation's. Rate yourself against these effective political skills:

▸ challenging destructive behaviour that goes against business and customer needs
▸ influencing others for the benefit of the organisation
▸ building alliances to achieve organisational objectives
▸ being ethical.

Chapter 6
Managing My Relationships

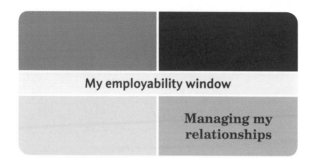

> What people skills do employers need?
>
> How do I take the best of me and the best of other people to produce dynamic, fruitful relationships?
>
> How can I demonstrate that my people skills will serve this employer's needs?

The final window pane is probably the most important. Exploring the first three panes sets you up to deploy your talents for optimum impact. This is the bit that other people will see. How well you do it is the focus of this chapter and is part of the *Doing it Well* phase.

Positive attitude

The starting position for some people is to see the good in others. Other people tend towards being judgemental. As you are now aware, our personality types allow us to view the world through different lenses, some of which we favour more than others. However, I stress again, they don't dictate how we behave, which is a choice based on awareness and developing ourselves to act skilfully.

Becoming aware of our potential can start at an early age through a coaching approach. I have been a business volunteer at an inner-city secondary school supporting young people in developing their entrepreneurial potential. The following is an illustration of behaviour change through the encouragement of a positive attitude.

> Imagine the scene. Forty 13- and 14-year-olds in a room for an Enterprise Day and half a dozen adult volunteers. My group of seven had six girls and one boy. I was their mentor for the day, helping them complete a scenario which involved setting up and running their own business. Part of my role was to give each person feedback after every round of the exercise.
>
> George has started the day on the wrong foot. Julie had been teasing him mercilessly, which egged the others on, so he folded his arms, sat back sullenly and disengaged. ▶

He would go wandering off during some of the activities. Julie had been particularly disruptive at every stage and Emma, playing the 'manager' of the business, was struggling to lead the team.

Then, something significant happened. The group had to make someone redundant and Julie volunteered ("I want to go on benefits, I don't want to work, I want to be a celebrity"). The group decided to change the manager and Jackie took over. She had excellent leadership skills and without the negative influence of Julie, the team started to engage, including George. By the end, he had come up with a great advertising poster that resulted in additional sales.

During the final feedback session, George admitted that he had quite enjoyed the day. With a smile, I reminded him of how the day started. "Which George do you want to be? The one at the start with your lip hanging out or the creative one who helped the team do so well?" He smiled back.

The attitude we choose to bring with us influences the response of the other person. Take the simple act of smiling. We tend to use phrases like 'a smile costs you nothing' or 'what have you got to lose?' based on negative assumptions about the threat of loss being a more important driver than gain. You don't often hear someone say 'what have you got to gain?'

Here's another example I observed when out shopping in a supermarket:

Lidl is a great place to shop. Whenever I go there, it's always full of weird surprises for sale like a trumpet or wet suits. The one I go to is frequented by an array of people of all nationalities, origins and classes. I find it an incredibly friendly place where people say hello, smile and joke with you in the queue. On this occasion, there were only two people on the checkouts and the line soon built up. Yet, the banter that flowed, the good-natured shouting across the aisles to check the price of some obscure item and the general lightness of the atmosphere meant that no one complained, or got annoyed or irritable at having to wait. Customers started joining in the banter!

It got me thinking about the unconscious, natural skills of the check-out staff on that day in managing potential conflict and delivering customer service. Although they may not recognise these talents explicitly (or even care much), they played to their strengths of charm, patience, good humour and a positive attitude resulting in a 'we're OK' scenario.

My supermarket anecdote reflects an interesting piece of research by the University of Warwick's Business School (11 July 2010, *The Observer*) led by a leading authority on the relationship between economics and mental health. It suggests there are clear links between workers' happiness and their productivity and that positive emotions have been an often overlooked ingredient.

The School of Life is behind an emerging mass movement called Action for Happiness (www.actionforhappiness.org), which advocates a radical change towards a more caring society based on *"the well-established finding that those who do things to make others happy become happier themselves"*.

Working in a team

Why does teamworking matter to employers? What do they prize or value? What do they want from you? How can you demonstrate you have what they need or the potential to add something?

However independent we may prefer to be, at some point in our working lives, we will find ourselves working in a team. The hugely varied nature of that experience can sometimes mask the common factors and features that are needed for a successful team. We don't always recognise that we have deployed good team skills and behaviours because of the labels we or other people put on our experience.

For example, imagine the following scenario with a teenager we'll call Jon:

> *How good are you at teamworking?*
> Jon: I don't know.
>
> *OK, what do you like doing best, Jon?*
> Jon: Playing football.
>
> *What position do you play?*
> Jon: Midfield. I'm the captain as well.
>
> *What do you do as the captain?*
> Jon: I'm always talking to the team. We do a group huddle just before the start and I remind them what I expect today. We win and lose together. I encourage the lads when we're losing and it's great when we win. When we score a goal, everyone celebrates by jumping on the scorer.
>
> *How does that make you feel?*
> Jon: I get a great deal of pleasure out of seeing the lads respond. They know when to step up to the plate and when they're having a stinker. They're not afraid to give their views or ideas to me. I feel respected.
>
> *What impact does that have on results?*
> Jon: It definitely helps. We've created a good bond between us so people are more up for it and it translates into their performances. I've been in teams before where the relationship isn't right and it's obvious from the results.

It can be hard to make explicit connections between what we take for granted and putting it in a way that relates to what an employer is seeking. Another person can free up your thinking by adopting a coaching approach to support you in exploring and making sense of your experience.

It also means you need an understanding of the key features and characteristics of teamworking – what it looks like and the commonly used terms within organisations. Employers will often have their own slant on teamworking within their organisation. They will want to know if you will fit in to their particular teamworking ethos – the skills, knowledge, attitudes and behaviours that support being a team player.

Employers often express this in an explicit organisational value. For example, on their website the Royal Shakespeare Company refers to the way they do things as Ensemble – *"We believe that dynamic, distinctive theatre is made by working together with trust and mutual respect – that the whole is greater than the sum of its parts"* (www.rsc.org.uk). It applies to both actors and the staff who work there.

Your own experiences and values will shape what you believe makes a good team member. We tend to act based on our map of the world and we can struggle when other people's maps don't match ours. Try this little thought experiment – *'A good team member is one that…'* and check what has influenced your response.

The starting point for understanding how to work effectively in any real team is to ask yourself – Who am I? Who are you? Who are we? What are we here to do? How will we achieve it? You have an opportunity to use your personal preferences to be at your best when working in a team. The trick is to spot where you can contribute most effectively and rewardingly.

In Chapter 4, I talked about preferences – what we naturally gravitate to, resulting in a pattern of tendencies that we take through life (like being right- or left-handed). These are not abilities (we can use our other hand) as they result from developing our competence, the basis for which is being an effective learner. For example, Rafael Nadal is right-handed but plays tennis with his left. In the 1970s, Wimbledon Champion Margaret Court was taught to play left handed by tying her right arm behind her back because it gave her an advantage over other players.

Researchers have long since identified a cluster of behaviours that we like to contribute or interrelate when in a team. The labels differ as academics and consultants have to make a living! Here are some common ones based on a workbook from Finding Potential (see Appendix 2). As you read through them, make a note of the ones that best fit you and those that clearly do not:

Chair	Networker
Takes charge, brings order, purpose and structure to the group, focuses on group processes	Gregarious and engaging, has many contacts in the organisation. Brings in external resources to the team
Driver	**Perfectionist**
Pushes for action and results. Promotes initiatives, independent and determined. Focuses on the team goal	Focused on detail and rules. Intolerant of the slapdash and casual, finds errors that others have missed
Innovator	**Team Player**
Imaginative and insightful. Concerned with the essential issues and the source of the team's essential ideas	Friendly and empathetic. Promotes team harmony. Listens and supports others
Critic	**Implementer**
Analytical and challenging, picks up flaws in arguments and stops team from pursuing unrealistic objectives	Disciplined, organised and reliable. Works hard to ensure the objectives of the team are realised

Remember, an overplayed strength often becomes a weakness. So, drive too much and other team members will see you as too pressurising; be too much of a perfectionist and you will be seen as pedantic. Other people will come to expect and tolerate some of these overplayed behaviours from you – but only up to a point!

You may find you like to contribute two or three of these roles. Whether you actually contribute them in practice will depend on what you negotiate with other people who may wish to do the same. If everyone played the critic, it would be a pretty depressing team atmosphere. Too many implementers and no driver or innovator, the team might struggle to identify the best option and get going in the right direction. A team full of networkers might have great meetings or never meet at all! The key point is to have the conversation in the first place.

Therefore, being at your best in a team involves assessing how you like to contribute, making that known to the team, establishing others' preferences, negotiating when and where to best contribute and continually developing your capability in the way you deploy those behaviours.

 You may have had more poor than good experiences of teamworking or vice versa. Put that aside and think about when it was motivating and rewarding and you succeeded in bridging the gap between you and others in the team. It might be an amalgam of different experiences.

▸ What made it brilliant?

▸ What did you/other people do?

▸ How did that make you feel?

▸ How did you contribute to the balance of the team?

▸ What impact did it have on achieving the team's goal?

Here is one definition of a high-performing team with six basic elements to help you think about it further:

> **A small number of people (generally fewer than twelve) with complementary skills, a common purpose, a common set of specific performance goals, a commonly agreed upon working approach and who hold each other mutually accountable for performance**
>
> Jon Katzenbach and Douglas Smith

Knowing when to lead and when to follow is another aspect of being a good teamworker. As you can see from the different team roles, each contribution is likely to come to the forefront at different times. You are taking the lead at that time irrespective of whether you occupy a formally appointed team leader position. At other times you will take a back seat and follow. 'Following' is an effective 'training ground' to prepare for future leadership opportunities. It requires balance, flexibility and a lot of self-management.

> **Followers who tell the truth, and leaders who listen to it, are an unbeatable combination**
>
> Warren Bennis, leadership author

 What does being a good follower or team player look like? Here are some common attributes, qualities and behaviours:

- the individual desire to serve others and support a team in its task to complete a goal
- helping the leaders become more effective while remaining true to your own values and essential needs
- knowing what you are expected to do, having clarity about your role and those of others
- making things happen, taking the initiative, contributing to discussions and keeping leaders informed
- supporting leaders' efforts to generate positive change
- maintaining co-operative working relationships, negotiating/persuading and maintaining an awareness of the interdependence with others
- acting with integrity by respecting others, being honest with yourself and holding yourself accountable, doing what you promise, being open with others
- helping other leaders to fully utilise their strengths and compensate for or overcome their weaknesses
- providing constructive disagreement that helps to balance other leaders' extremes
- speaking out when it is necessary to do so, such as by challenging leaders' flawed plans or strategies and getting on with it once a decision has been made
- skilfully developing a high level of respect and mutual trust with leaders so as to offer them a balanced or differing perspective
- showing leaders appropriate appreciation and recognition
- not simply complaining about leaders, but helping them to become better ones
- recognising that assisting a weak leader can help you to develop critical leadership skills of your own.

What are you going to continue doing? Do more of? Start doing? What is your unique offer to employers in terms of teamworking? How does it help meet their needs?

The more skilled and competent you become in teamworking, the quicker you can hit the ground running when you join a new team. A study in 2010 by workplace psychologists OPP says that being a successful multi-team player is down to personality, and this has the biggest impact on the effectiveness of these teams. We are all unique individuals so understanding the differences and similarities between you and your fellow team members will help you nip conflict in the bud or deal with it in alternative ways.

Being a good teamworker is not always easy. It depends on the culture of the section/ organisation and the situation. For example, in hierarchies where position is power and performance management is poor, the result can be inappropriate behaviours by managers. In the current climate of redundancies, the pressures on those that remain can have a distorting effect on some individuals at the cost of healthy relationships and business success. Here's the Buddha's take on having 'nous':

> **Believe nothing, no matter where you read it, or who said it, no matter if I have said it, unless it agrees with your own reason and your own common sense**
>
> Siddhartha Gautama

Communicating

Improving communication, especially internally, has been a bugbear of staff in every organisation where I have been employed or which I have worked alongside as consultant, coach or trainer. Staff surveys are littered with communication questions so it can sometimes feel like a self-fulfilling exercise. They cover everything from organisation-wide communication systems and processes to personal skills and capability.

There are three basic elements.– the message (what), the medium (how) and the people involved – the sender and the receiver (who). Society is going through an era of transition for all of them:

▸ **Message** – The search for meaning in our lives in an increasingly fragmented world. What is your 'message' (unique offer) to employers? What do you want to say about your values, beliefs, motivations and goals? What are employers saying they need in these tough times? How good is the match?

▸ **Medium** – Use of the Internet and social media has gone mainstream. In what ways are employers and their customers/users communicating? How well do you communicate in person and using different technology/social media? What are employers asking for? What skills and behaviours do you need to get your message across?

▸ **People** – Demographic changes now mean there are more older workers than younger ones in the workplace. Who will you communicate with in this job or role? What are the implications for you in communicating effectively with the other three generations in the workplace alongside your own?

Relationship Theory (see Appendix 2) starts from the premise that everyone wants to feel worthwhile about themselves as human beings. We get our self-esteem from being valued by others for the things we wish to be valued for. As you have seen, your motivation is internally driven and your behaviour is your way of reflecting your intentions (self-perception). When other people see your external behaviours, they make judgements about your intentions and therefore your motivation (their perception of you).

What you are trying to do and what they are seeing you do doesn't always match up. This can lead to misunderstandings and conflict. We go into conflict when things are important to us. When we witness conflict between other people, we learn what is important to them.

Therefore, how well you communicate is a function of knowing what motivates you, an understanding of your values, skill in articulating your intentions, accurately reading the intentions of other people based on what motivates them and skilful self-management of your response.

Employers want effective communicators who listen and question well because they build rapport, empathy and healthy and productive relationships with other people to achieve what the business requires.

They also want people who can put their point of view across coherently, fluently and confidently or who have, as the CBI label it, oral literacy.

Listening well

'Active listening' has become a hackneyed phrase. Prefacing listening with the word 'active' has evolved because many people either don't listen or only hear what they want, best parodied by the expression 'I hear what you say...'

So what does listening well look like?

Listening is about what we pay attention to when interacting with another person. It's about listening with genuine respect and interest so that you have a positive effect on them.

> **The quality of your attention determines the quality of other people's thinking**
>
> Nancy Kline

In my experience, too many people default to making statements about themselves or their issues and neglect genuinely seeking to understand the other person's position through skilful listening and questioning. Too many conversations end up in conflict when the rational and emotional minds conflict.

The UK electorate seemed to recognise this in the general election of 2010 when the majority of people articulated a desire for our politicians to listen more, to talk to each other more; for consensus rather than adversarial positioning.

True listening involves a mindset change from 'me' to 'you'. If your starting point is 'me', you will be listening to the imaginary parrot on your shoulder saying to you:

- ‣ What am I going to say next? What's my next question?
- ‣ I know what you're going to say next
- ‣ But…
- ‣ I believe I know best and I want to give you some advice
- ‣ Let me tell you about me and what I'm doing.

If your starting point is 'you', you will be paying attention to the three levels below.

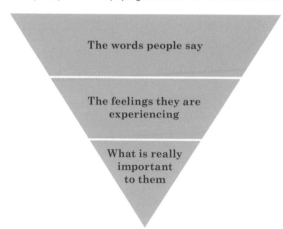

The first level is about making sense of the actual words people say: checking your understanding of information or facts, and taking account of the context and what the words are conveying on the surface in relation to the topic in hand. To show you are listening here involves summarising (using their words), paraphrasing (using your words), and clarifying, testing and affirming through appropriate body language (nodding, saying 'yes', mirroring them in your posture).

The second level is about observing whether the meaning of the words matches how the other person is actually feeling as they say them. Does the body language (tone, posture etc) match what is being said? To show you are listening may involve reflecting back how you are experiencing them and testing assumptions about body language (crossing arms may just be more comfortable for some people).

The third level is often about what the person is not saying. From what they say and how they are coming across, can you discern what is really important to them? This is about their personal values and beliefs. Listening here may involve reframing to ensure communication is clear and meaningful in terms of intended outcomes.

Here is a real example from a coaching conversation with a client we'll call Sue, based on an approach by Robert Kegan and Lisa Laskow Lahey:

> **The issue:** *What would you want to do differently or change?*
> Sue: I want to have a positive working relationship with my boss. He doesn't give me any recognition. It goes back to childhood as I've always sought approval from my father. ‣

The stated commitment: What underpinning beliefs are revealed in your statement?
Sue: Relationships at work and being valued for my achievements by an authority figure are important to me.
The self-limiting belief: What is it that you do or don't do that maintains the current situation?
Sue: I avoid addressing the issue.
The competing commitment: If you did the opposite, what would be your real concerns or anxieties?
Sue: Hurting or damaging him because he's weak and vulnerable or making him angry.
The big assumption: What are you protecting yourself from?
Sue: Conflict.
Therefore, what is your real challenge?
Sue: Overcoming my fear of conflict.
If you knew that you were not afraid of conflict, what could you do in this situation?
Sue: Not let things go by again, be more challenging and assertive.
When will you next have an opportunity to do this?
Sue: I am seeing him on Wednesday and will talk to him about his impact on me, how it makes me feel and what I want from him.
What specifically?
Sue: For him to acknowledge my contribution to the report he presents at the board meeting.
What else could you do?
Sue: Ask to attend with him and present the relevant bits.
On a scale of 1-10, how committed are you to doing this?
Sue: 10!
Ring me on Thursday and tell me how you have got on. (And she did phone to confirm she had taken action and the situation improved.)

Being more employable means dialogue rather than monologue. It means developing the skill and habit of testing each other's assumptions. An enhanced ability to genuinely listen is the basis for consciously entering into dialogue with an open mind about the other person or the issue in hand, and focusing hard and remaining in the present moment.

Where does most of your focus lie when you are communicating with someone – you or them? Do you find yourself interrupting others in mid-flow or often thinking about the next thing you want to say as they are speaking? How much interest do you show in their concerns through thoughtful questions? How do they know you have been listening?

When minds meet, they don't just exchange facts: they transform them, reshape them, draw different implications from them, engage in new trains of thought

Theodore Zeldin, philosopher

On a trip to an art museum in Dublin, I was greeted on arrival in the foyer by a rack of dozens of donated shoes of every imaginable shape, style, size and colour. You couldn't enter the museum unless you left your own shoes at the entrance and put on another pair from the rack. It was an odd sensation stepping into someone else's shoes (I deliberately chose something wacky) and it really made you wonder about the original owner. A truly empathetic experience.

When have you stepped into a customer's or user's 'shoes'? What did it feel like? What did you learn about the customer/user? Have you ever taken on somebody else's job or role for a day, or shadowed someone? What story could you tell to this employer to demonstrate your communication skills?

There is a scene in Mike Leigh's film *Happy Go Lucky* where the lead character meets a vagrant in a chance encounter that shows empathy in all its glorious shades – listening with her eyes, ears and voice to his half-articulated and painful memories. This is emotional connection at its rawest, just being there for someone rather than doing anything for them. Greater empathy for other people is surely one antidote to the increase of human solitude driven by our market-driven society, reported by the Mental Health Foundation.

To be a good listener is essential to being employable and requires our empathy to be authentic. You can't easily break down the steps involved in empathising as it is often instinctive, as the film scene exemplifies. If you have a natural knack for picking up on other people's feelings, then use it to listen well. If you don't, work on giving attention to the clues other people give.

You will also need maturity (defined by the behavioural psychologist, Rosemary Rowe, as "the ability to tolerate ambiguity") and a firm, sure touch in dealing with people and situations, or good old-fashioned judgement ("knowing me, knowing you", as the Abba song goes). It's a mix of being skilfully responsive and assertive.

Part of the skill is in choosing the behaviour that leads us to the result we want. Real listening involves giving up some control or power, some certainty and assumptions. To listen is more than a skill, it's also an attitude of mind. It is a value set that says what you have to say and how you feel is as important as my agenda. I may disagree, but I acknowledge your position and in my response I will factor in your considerations, otherwise I'm saying you don't matter enough to me.

Effective listening builds trust, and the key to nudging people towards trust is to place values and ethics at the centre of our conversations. The natural human response is to reciprocate and respond positively when someone shows faith in our abilities and our integrity. We build genuine relationships based on mutual trust through being authentic, true to ourselves, looking outwardly to the concerns and needs of other people, and engaging each other from a values-centred position. Overplayed or without skill, this becomes pious, preaching, bombastic or arrogant.

Questioning

> **You can tell whether a man is clever by his answers.**
> **You can tell whether a man is wise by his questions**
>
> Naguib Mahfouz, first Egyptian winner of the Nobel Prize for Literature

Effective communication skills for employability are also about asking the right questions at the right times in the right ways. The use of different types of questioning techniques depends on what you want to achieve from the question. Here are some types of questions, their purposes and where they may be useful or unhelpful.

Type of question	Purposes/where useful	Where unhelpful
Open 'Tell me about this role' What? When? Where? How? Who? Why? (see caveat in the unhelpful column)	▸ Most openings in a conversation ▸ Exploring new areas and to gather information ▸ Encouraging the other person to open up and then demonstrate your listening skills	▸ With over-talkative people or where clarification is required ▸ Be careful about your use of 'why?' It's OK in the right tone of voice where the relationship is good. If not, it can sometimes come across as judgemental or evaluative and lead to defensiveness. An alternative is to say 'What is behind that?' or 'What makes you say that?'
Probing 'Exactly what does that mean for my career?'	▸ Getting precise details ▸ Checking information	▸ If you want to explore emotionally charged areas
Closed 'What is the salary for this job?' 'So, are you saying that...?'	▸ Obtaining a fact ▸ Seeking a yes or no answer for clarification	▸ If you want to gain information in areas not yet fully explored ▸ If you want to get people to open up
Hypothetical 'What would happen if...?'	▸ Getting people to talk about new areas ▸ Reframing the issue ▸ Testing an idea or alternative situation in the future	▸ If there are non-negotiable or known and agreed constraints or boundaries

Type of question	Purposes/where useful	Where unhelpful
Leading 'I suppose you know what my strengths are from my CV don't you?' 'So that seems to be the answer then doesn't it?'	▸ Gaining acceptance of your view ▸ Playing devil's advocate to gauge response	▸ If you want to gain any information about the person or situation
Multiple 'What is your position on… and are you saying… or is it that…?'	▸ Never	▸ If you want clarity and a meaningful response

How well do you measure up to asking questions? Rate yourself against the list above in terms of your appropriate and inappropriate use of questions. What type of questioning approach will help move you towards your goals?

Oral literacy

Being orally literate gives you confidence and gives an employer confidence in you. It involves making yourself understood, being persuasive or influential, conveying your intent skilfully and authentically, and being assertive about your position while recognising the position of others. It links back to earlier sections on assertiveness and personal presentation.

The language we choose to use is important because it signals to others our respect for how they may like to receive information (detail? big picture?), so making it easier for them to relate to and therefore warm to us. It is also about what fits culturally within a given situation or organisation. Using jargon inappropriately or leaving it unexplained can affect how you are perceived.

In looking at what makes you and other people tick and making the most of yourself, we touched upon how different people like to communicate. You will need to adapt your communication style to fit the situation and the person or group in front of you.

What communication style or approach does this employer or person value? How do you know? What do you know about them already? How do you experience them in the moment? When do you need to hold back? When do you need to advocate your view and sell yourself? When is it more appropriate to listen or ask questions?

A challenge we all face is to clearly communicate our strengths and weaknesses to an employer. You don't want the best of you to be misunderstood nor to be on the defensive. The goal is to find the right language and to emphasise the positive.

Researchers and authors, Marcus Buckingham and Donald O. Clifton, make the point that *"the language of human weakness is rich and varied... the language of human strength is sparse"*. The danger with both is a tendency to generalise ('I'm poor at communicating', 'I've got great people skills') and they don't tell you very much.

Be specific on what you are good at and how they meet the needs of this role and employer. Everybody has areas that are not their natural strengths so avoid dismissing or minimising questions on them from employers. Where you have a relevant and significant weakness, present it in a way that makes clear under what conditions it occurs (it won't be all the time), how you manage it and any support you need. You can present a skill or knowledge gap as an opportunity to learn.

Give examples and tell compelling stories. For example, in a sales role, communicating could be broken down into excelling at building trust or being great at initiating contacts. If your strength is in leading other people, what does it mean precisely in terms of your unique experience and perspective? For example, is it being good at developing people or building a vision that people want to follow (or maybe both)?

Using the right language to demonstrate our trustworthiness is part of skilfully engaging other people. Author Simon Sinek says *"when articulating values, instead of 'integrity' say 'always doing the right thing'; instead of 'innovation' say 'looking at the problem from a different angle' ... as it's hard to hold people accountable to abstract nouns!"*

Remember, the aim is to create your unique offer that helps to differentiate you from other people. Revisit the relevant strengths you identified earlier and practice different ways you can articulate them with assurance and appropriate pride.

Writing

The CBI says employers want people who are able to produce clear, structured written work. If you are employed, how you write reflects on you and the company. If you are seeking a job, the quality of your CV is crucial. What constitutes 'written' is a moot point given the wide choice of formats that modern technology now gives us. The message, the medium and the audience affects why, what and how we communicate using the written word.

Here are some considerations, whatever your circumstances:

▸ When is something in writing appropriate rather than a conversation (and vice versa)? Facts, information and records are all suitable for a written format. Where the 'tone' is critical, such as conveying strong emotions or giving personal feedback, it is better done in person to allow for instant clarification and avoid misinterpretation.

▸ What level of formality does this message need to have?

▸ What style of writing is appropriate for this audience and this purpose? Good grammar will matter to some employers whereas others may take a more relaxed view. If the role or job involves attention to detail, you will need to reflect that in all your written communication with a prospective or existing employer.

▸ Reports, email, texts, instant messaging, tweets, blogs, wikis, online application forms, CVs, resumes, sales material, advertising/sales/marketing/press release copy etc all have their own idiosyncrasies and contexts. Where possible, become aware of the prevailing way things are done for that employer or specific sections and individuals. What do you know already? What do you need to find out? How and when will you do that?

▸ Literacy expert, Diane Hall of The Writing Hall (www.thewritinghall.co.uk), suggests *"a flawless, effective, accurate and proofread CV is a must in the first instance. Unless you're known to the hirer and they can look past poor literacy skills for other personal assets, your CV will be your 'shop-front' and is all the employer has to go on. Poor literacy detracts from the main message, just as much as a stutter or nerves in speech and negative body language"*.

▸ Jargon is a challenge and an opportunity. Use employer- or sector-specific language that is standard or accepted and avoid trying to impress with vague or fashionable buzzwords. Use plain English wherever possible. Take a look at *The Sun* newspaper and its style and use of words. It is clear, punchy and unambiguous. Does your written work do what it says on the tin? As Einstein wisely commented, *"If you can't explain it simply, you don't understand it well enough"*.

▸ One avenue to explore is to get a professional literacy coach or mentor who can support your development in literacy and expression or provide a writing critique/evaluation service to ensure your material is accurate and fit for purpose. For example, see www.thewritinghall.co.uk.

The Internet and social media

This idea of always being 'on', 'connected' or 'wired' is seriously changing the way we live our lives. I read in the *London Evening Standard* (23 August 2010) of a woman who had got rid of all her CDs, DVDs, TV, books etc and just used her laptop plus an iPad. No need for separate hard drives either as she backed everything up in the 'cloud'. Another guy had sold his flat and possessions and was now happily living in hotels via laterooms.com at a cheaper rate than his monthly mortgage payments.

For the current generation, communicating via the Internet and using social media is something they have grown up with and use as part of their daily lives at home or at work. For older generations the learning curve has been steeper. Many have embraced the tools, if not always the mindset. Yet, I believe it cannot be avoided to be employable now and in the future.

I find myself living between old and new ways almost without realising it. My mobile now notifies me every time a text, voicemail or email is received. The entire contents of my laptop are backed up into cyberspace every week without me lifting so much as a digit. I can liaise real time with any number of online, 24/7 help desks. My blog is primed to deliver automatically at a date of my choosing. Virtual office admin freelancers are a thriving industry so you can task, delegate or direct and know things will get done while you sleep.

You can even buy a pen that records audio at the same time, then click on any word you have written and it takes you to exactly the same place on the recording, as well as download to your laptop and the text magically appears (www.livescribe.com). The Martini effect is alive and well – anytime, anyplace, anywhere!

I am not alone. According to recent news reports, we all now spend 50% of our daily waking hours 'connected' to our mobiles, computers and TVs. What we're all looking at is another matter. The twitterati are debating if our brains are being rewired by this constant digital interaction. Educationalists worry that this generation has a smaller attention span than previous ones. People can't sleep because of the perpetual noise of data and information in their heads. I read a review of a book recently about writer Tim Parks' increasing ill-health over a number of years – he kept getting serious and unexplained intestinal pains. He discovered that the cure was to stop 'thinking' so much and start experiencing the moment more at a spiritual, emotional and physical level.

So what does this tell us about being employable, the nature of change and our ability to embrace it healthily and assertively? We will all need to go with the flow, learn new skills, develop better personal stress management strategies, discover, be courageous, adapt or become obsolete.

What can you do now to embrace the digital revolution to be more employable? Your starting point will depend on your computer skills, familiarity and skill level with information and social communication technology. Avoided it so far? What's stopping you from engaging? Jane Bozarth, a world expert in the use of social media in training, defines social media as a means of dissemination of information by the public to a community that invites interaction. The advantages of popular ones like Facebook and YouTube are that they are free, easy to use and enable learners to stay connected.

Here are some ideas to support you being more employable:

- Create your personal brand online through, for example, LinkedIn, which has become an essential site for professionals to promote themselves and their businesses. A recent poll on LinkedIn found that, out of over 1000 respondents, nearly 80% said they had been contacted for a job opportunity.

- Seek opportunities on sector-specific jobsites by registering and uploading tailored CVs.

- Develop an awareness of relevant search engines for finding the information you need to reach your goals including Google and their competitors. Twitter can give you answers instantly and concisely in no more than 140 characters. Identify useful resources that match your preferences and needs such as YouTube, Wikipedia, interesting websites, podcasts, webinars and blogs in your field of expertise or sector/industry. Maintain a manageable number of RSS feeds (Really Simple Syndication) to keep you updated. These are a way of being notified when there is an update from your favourite site.

- Direct mail expert, John Bartlett, suggests putting QR codes on your CV or resume. Google 'free QR codes from Google' and/or 'QR code reader'. You create an image that is scannable by a smart phone that sends the person to a website. Then go to a 'build a free website' site and put your resume on there and any additional things that don't fit on a resume (like your picture or scanned-in awards etc). When an employer or recruiter scans the QR code, it will pull up your resume website on their phone. You can also put your QR code on the back of a business card making it easy for companies to view your information with just a scan of their smartphone. That will show you are technically savvy, up on the latest technology and it is something a little different than most that may help them remember you.

- Join relevant online forums and learning communities in your area of expertise and contribute to discussions in order to establish your presence, to demonstrate your goodwill by offering or responding to something for nothing, to ask questions and to learn from others.

- Start to become familiar or stay up to date with developing tools and technologies to stay connected, make your working life more efficient and develop new capabilities to offer current or future employers. For example, take a look at The Centre for Learning and Performance Technologies' annual 100 top learning tools and emerging trends at www.c4lpt.co.uk and be selective.

Networking

Networking is one of those ideas like Marmite – you either love it or hate it. Some people are negative about networking based on potentially outdated perceptions or experiences, such as that it's only about excruciating events with a bunch of strangers. It can easily seem to be time-consuming and a wasted effort without the confidence and tools to be effective.

The ways in which people are now networking and the value it brings are changing, partly because of technology and partly the imperative of finding jobs or staying in work in an era of rising unemployment. Networking has become essential to being more employable, whether within or external to an organisation, and it can no longer be left to chance.

It requires a positive, 'can do' attitude and many of the other skills and behaviours already covered. Neil Munz-Jones, in his book *The Reluctant Networker*, makes the point that it's about developing a networking 'style' that suits your personality and plays to your strengths and how you prefer to do things. At the heart of good networking are relationships and the quality of your engagement and communication.

Here's an example from business communication coach and champion for introverts, Nancy Ancowitz, who asked a client which of his strengths as an introvert he's used in approaching his job search. *"My abilities to research, work independently, and think deeply to evaluate some of the major issues faced by companies during the downturn (and) I've been reconnecting with people from my network individually"*.

The reasons for networking in order to be more employable include:

▸ helping you to find the right direction of travel for your career

▸ gaining access to the unadvertised jobs market and more of the right roles to fit your unique offer

▸ sharing information and learning to help you achieve your own and other people's goals

▸ raising your profile in your field of expertise

▸ deepening existing relationships

▸ building genuine, trusting relationships with relevant people for mutual benefit

▸ increasing your business and customer awareness

▸ enhancing success in your current role.

Neil Munz-Jones' top 10 tips for networking at www.changeboard.com, based on his book *The Reluctant Networker*:

▶ **Make it easy for people to help you**
People are busy so be clear on what kind of roles interest you, make your pitch succinct and memorable.

▶ **Be clear on who you want to network with**
Who do you want to spend time with? Who is likely to help you because they know you and would be willing to recommend you?

▶ **Become an expert in your field**
So that when people need specific help they think of you.

▶ **Are you making the most of LinkedIn?**
Four million UK members, and growing, reconnect with former contacts, keep in touch, have a full profile and update regularly; follow organisations that interest you and get introductions through your growing network.

▶ **Spend more time in coffee shops**
Don't like going to events and meeting new people? Make time for coffee or lunch with existing contacts and deepen the relationship.

▶ **Make the most of networking events**
Be selective, target relevant ones likely to be attended by the people you want to connect with, come prepared and remember to be you. It's not about selling, it's about trust-building.

▶ **Get speaking!**
Find a subject on which you are an expert and offer to speak. Invite along some of your contacts.

▶ **Are you making the most of your company's marketing?**
Find a reason to stay in touch by forwarding interesting articles, materials or links and inviting contacts to events.

▶ **Get in the habit of catch-up calls**
When did you last speak to people on your contacts list? Call them and share how things are and what's on your respective plates.

▶ **How can I help?**
Find it awkward asking people for help? Feel good by helping others with interesting articles, people for them to meet or career opportunities. Genuine and positive relationships tend to result in reciprocal behaviour.

Heather Townsend, author of *The Financial Times Guide to Business Networking*, uses the marketing analogy of a 'personal brand' – *"With online networking enabling people to maintain networks ten to one hundred times bigger than five years ago, it's your personal brand which will be the difference between you getting the referral or someone else..."*.

According to *The Guardian* (29 January 2011), companies are recognising the importance of networking as well by increasingly seeking out graduates rather than waiting for them to apply. Careers fairs and campus presentations have now overtaken brochures and websites as the favoured means for firms to attract applicants. Many intend to appeal to promising students earlier in their university career with offers of work experience, open days and internships. If you are a recent graduate and you have worked there before, it may increase your chances of a permanent job.

If organisations can pick and choose from so many qualified (sometimes over-qualified) people, what is going to make you stand out? For me, it has to be you, the person. Getting that across on paper/online is a challenge. Networking skills and mindset are becoming more crucial. It's about using diverse approaches to create your own critical path, developed from a foundation of self-awareness and using those insights to match your unique offer to what a specific employer needs.

Solving problems

For the CBI, solving problems is about analysing facts and situations and applying creative thinking to develop appropriate solutions. For me, it also includes working collaboratively. As will have become clear from this book, some of the other employability elements are related, such as a 'can do' attitude and business and customer awareness. What then is distinct about solving problems?

At the outset, I explained that my approach is solution-focused rather than problem-centred. This was not meant to minimise or dismiss the idea that there are both small and significant problems to be addressed and overcome in the workplace or obstacles to being more employable (such as the availability of jobs in the current climate). However, we do have choices in how we tackle them. This section outlines alternative approaches and you can decide which you prefer or if you see merits in both.

> **If you shine strong light on one side of a problem, it casts long shadows on the other...**
>
> Wittgenstein

The standard approach to solving problems usually follows a linear sequence based on cause and effect, as follows:

- *identify* the problem
- *analyse* the root causes of the problem
- *determine* solutions to the problem
- *analyse* the solutions
- *select* the best solution to the problem
- *develop* an action plan to implement the solution.

This adheres to a rational, analytical approach to tackling a problem. This suits some personalities and the culture of many organisations, especially within technical or scientific communities.

Intellectuals solve problems, geniuses prevent them

Albert Einstein

You can apply this approach to being more employable. Here's a mock illustration:

- My problem is I'm in my 50s and I don't use social media.
- I have analysed the root causes of the problem and concluded that it is a combination of fear of the unknown and not knowing where to start.
- As a result, I am developing a strategy that includes different possible solutions to the problem. For example, I'm thinking of getting a friend/colleague who knows about this stuff to teach me, or going on a seminar/training course, or teaching myself, or... etc.
- I have done some research, looked at the pros and cons, including time and costs, and drawn some conclusions.
- It is now clear to me which solution best suits my situation and learning style.
- I have developed a plan of action of what I'm going to do to make this happen and when.

Now let's look at an alternative approach that turns the notion of a 'problem' on its head. One of the problems with problems is that they are a real downer. Remember the goal mapping approach that started with the end in mind? Success, even imagined, can bring the feelgood factor. It can sometimes feel more liberating and motivating if we start by accentuating the positive.

What that means in practice is the following:

- *Discover* what is working well, build from what is in place and has been proven to be successful (the best of what is)
- *Identify* factors that help you/the team/the organisation to work well and identify what could be replicated (why is it working?)
- *Create* a vision of what you/the team/the organisation is doing that causes it to be successful. What would it look like? (what might be)
- *Create* a dialogue that allows honest and open inquiry into all perspectives of the vision (let's road test our assumptions)
- *Select* the current factors of your own/the team's/the organisation's strength that can be leveraged to create the vision. What do we get behind? (what should be)
- *Develop* an action plan that uses the leverage points found in these factors of your own/ team/organisational strength to create the vision, and deliver (what will be).

Translated into the earlier example, it might look like this:

▸ I'm in my 50s and, although I don't use social media, I have been to a lot of business events, enjoy them and brought back some good practices and contacts for others to pursue.

▸ I have identified that it is my expertise in our field of work, the breadth of my experience and my affable nature that help me to work well at these events.

▸ I have imagined a situation where I can replicate some of these things online. Although it will stretch me, I can see myself illustrating my expertise, publishing testimonials, highlighting relevant experience in various profiles and still being able to meet people in person through the connections I grow.

▸ I have consulted with a few friends and colleagues to tease out some of my assumptions and get their perspective and ideas.

▸ It is now clear to me who can help me and how I can make this happen.

▸ I have developed a plan of action of what I'm going to do and when. I will know when I've achieved it and what my success looks like.

Maybe the difference between these two approaches is realism and optimism, and real life tends to require a bit of both. You can apply these approaches to any issue or challenge you face.

What stories can you tell an employer that demonstrates your ability to solve problems or find solutions?

Creativity

An integral element of solving problems or finding solutions is creativity. People often say they are not creative. Creativity tends to be associated with flamboyant, out-of-the-ordinary, original ideas, and some people tend to perpetuate their personal myths, as we explored earlier, in this area, too ('It's what other people do').

The reality is that creativity is a set of behaviours and skills that can be learned. Very few ideas are truly original as they tend to have their origins in what already exists.

Creativity is applied imagination

Sir Ken Robinson

Here are some common creativity techniques that you can apply and adapt to increase customer satisfaction and loyalty. Try using them to generate potential ideas that may play out in the marketplace.

- find an alternative way of describing or experiencing the service (what if...?)
- find an alternative but similar service or benefit in another field
- identify then deliberately challenge the rules and assumptions
- picture the opposite of the situation by reversing the objective
- use a deliberate connection with a random item
- think backwards, start with the desired solution
- look at the problem from the third-party or Martian point of view
- look at the problem through the innocence of a child.

You may be seen as competent in creativity within an organisation if you:

- develop new insights into situations and apply innovative solutions to make organisational improvements
- help to create a work environment that encourages creative thinking and innovation
- design and implement new ways of doing things.

What examples can you provide to a prospective or existing employer of where you have demonstrated any of the above?

Innovation involves the combination of being creative and taking calculated risks. When have you tried out something for the first time to meet a customer or user need? When have you tested a new way of working? What got adopted, introduced or implemented? How did you contribute?

> **Creativity only becomes innovation when ideas become useful. How can I make this real right now? Don't think, just leap!**
>
> Sticky Wisdom

Working collaboratively

The workplace will be increasingly collaborative, driven by technological opportunities to share and engage, and by new ways of working to get things done more efficiently and creatively in an era of austerity.

It goes beyond teamworking, which is confined by specific boundaries, although it shares some of its core elements. Collaboration crosses boundaries. We usually collaborate with someone to meet a joint objective, solve a problem or find a solution. It could be a colleague, a partner, another organisation, a customer or a supplier.

At the heart of working collaboratively is the issue of trust. The way you complete the following short personal audit from John Doyle at b2bppm.com will depend upon your situation. Think of some people and check out the level of trust with them by getting them to complete the audit too; then compare your results:

Trust Audit

1 = Strongly Disagree   **3** = Somewhat Disagree   **5** = Agree
2 = Disagree   **4** = Somewhat Agree   **6** = Strongly Agree

	Statement	My Score	Person A	My Score	Person B	My Score	Person C
1	When I agree to deliver something, I do so						
2	I listen to, and strive to understand, my colleague's point of view even if I disagree with it						
3	I demonstrate that I believe our relationship is of value to me						
4	I demonstrate appropriate knowledge in appropriate circumstances						
5	I say what I honestly think and feel						
6	I work through problems and challenges in a way designed to maintain collaboration						
7	I give honest feedback, even when it is difficult						
8	I seek to deliver outputs to time, quality and specification						
9	I have confidence in the decisions my colleague makes						
10	When my colleague tells me something, I am confident it is true						
11	I learn from my colleague						
12	I am willing to invest time and energy to maintain my relationship						

	Statement	My Score	Person A	My Score	Person B	My Score	Person C
13	My colleague listens to, and considers, my feedback when offered						
14	I do not exaggerate to make myself look good or expert						
15	I can tell my colleague things that are sensitive						

Why is this relationship important to you? If the relationship is positive, what contributes to this? If it is negative, what contributes to this?

Part of trust-building is formed by some of the factors already mentioned, such as how open or closed you are, how much you seek feedback or provide it to others, how you deal with conflict constructively, being assertive in a way that respects your position and the person(s) with whom you are collaborating and how comfortable you are with interdependence.

The Hay Group suggest the mindset is one of intolerance of boundaries, avoidance of protectionism and being prepared to ask 'why not?' The focus is on the result – solving a problem or finding a solution – through a trusting, mutually beneficial relationship (www.publicservice.co.uk).

Numeracy

Being numerate is about the ability to make basic calculations, such as working out a percentage. It is also about understanding some common mathematical principles behind the workings of everyday life and their implications for being more employable.

People often wear *innumeracy* as a badge of honour. 'I was never any good at maths', 'I'm more of a people person'. Expect eyes to light up if you say you're numerate and don't be surprised if they only mean 'can you add up, take away and multiply?'

Innumeracy is defined by maths professor John Allen Paulos as *"an inability to deal comfortably with the fundamental notions of number and chance"*. The consequences are not always obvious, yet innumeracy can result in horrendous misassumptions about the behaviour of other people, including miscarriages of justice (how juries vote).

Here are a couple of the consequences that being innumerate can have:

▸ *Inappropriate adding:* If you have a 50% chance of getting the job on a Monday and 50% chance on a Tuesday, it does not mean you have a 100% chance!

▸ *The urge to average:* Your boss tells you that are on a waiting list for a promotion and the average waiting time is 5 months. If this is all you know, you might be hopeful. Maybe two-thirds of the others on the waiting list won't get promoted within a month. Maybe the lucky third get promoted within a month. You only know the average time and not the distribution waiting times before promotion happens.

Recognition has been given by mathematicians that their profession does not make life easy for us mere mortals (see – now I'm doing it). The language and perceived complexity mean that some of us struggle with the vagaries of mathematical principles as opposed to straightforward, black and white answers based on the simplistic view that 2 + 2 must always equal 4.

On the other hand, mathematicians get frustrated at our lack of respect for numbers and chance compared with language and the use of grammar. Paulos cites the examples of obsessions with 'continuous v continually' and 'imply v infer' (look them up if you don't know).

 Some of the lack of understanding is to do with our psychological need to be certain, and therefore intolerance of uncertainty or ambiguity, and a belief in coincidence and how a problem is framed. Here are some common examples (by no means exhaustive) adapted from the work of Paulos and how they relate to some broad employability issues:

- **Personalising:** The number of people who die in aeroplanes v who die in car crashes – a common response to the former by the innumerate is to personalise ('but what if you're that one?'). The number of people who will apply for this job v you getting an interview or the job itself ('why would it be me?'). Why not you?

- **Magnitudes:** The difference between a million and a billion (eg it takes 11.5 days for a million seconds to elapse v 32 years for a billion seconds tick away). Think bankers' bonuses or the size of the national debt. One graduate chasing, on average, 100–120 posts (Association of Graduate Recruiters, 2011) v 20% of recent graduates actively seeking work (Office for National Statistics, 2011).

- **Scaling** numbers up or down proportionally is often invalid. If the number of available jobs goes up by 5%, it doesn't mean 5% of unemployed people will apply or be able to apply. If the size of a company doubles, it doesn't mean the size of its departments will also double in size.

- **Calculating large numbers:** As consultant and meetings expert Patrick Lencioni explains in his book *Death by Meeting*, if there are 16 members in a team, it means 120 possible combinations of one-to-one relationships that have to be maintained to keep everyone on the same page. A team of 7 has 21. Think of the number of people that report to the team and the communication challenge increases dramatically.

- **Probabilities:** The probability of getting two heads in two flips of a coin is 1 in 4. Five straight coin flips coming up heads is 1 in 32. The probability that someone chosen at random was not born in June is 11 in 12. The probability that none of 12 randomly selected people was born in June is 35.2%. A 20% chance of rain implies an 80% chance of no rain.

  In Chapter 4, what was the probability of Amy of getting an interview for the job where there were 80 interview places and 2300 applicants? What was the probability of her getting one of the 12 jobs on offer at the start and then after being selected for interview? (The answers are at the end of this section on page 130).

- **Coincidences:** Innumerate people tend to underestimate the frequency of coincidences and endlessly try to rationalise things that seem to correspond. If you anticipate another person's thoughts or have a dream that seems to come true, many would put this down to the mysterious workings of the universe. The reality is that while an unfortunate event may well occur (the train gets cancelled), there is much less chance that a particular one will (the 7.20am on the day of the interview).

- **Chance:** The value or opportunity presented to you by the contacts you make on LinkedIn are based on the idea of the number of degrees of separation between you and other people in a chain of connections. So, you might have a modest 60 contacts which translates to a potential 7900 connections two degrees away (friends of friends) and 771,200 connections three degrees away (friends of their friends). Therefore, the likelihood of you and a stranger meeting, say at a business conference, and being linked via two intermediaries in between is unexpectedly high (irrespective of whether or not you have the conversation that happens to uncover your mutual friendship – I can it hear it now: 'well, isn't it a small world, what are the chances of that?').

- **Significance:** Statistical significance has a different meaning from how we use the word 'significance' in everyday language. Through calculating the standard deviation, significance means we are confident that something cannot be down to chance alone. It doesn't tell you why. The most common error is for an organisation to say, for example, that their productivity or profits or the arrest rates for burglary have gone up by 10% this year without giving any context. On the face of it, you think it is good news. Then you discover that the year before it had gone up 40% and the year before that 2% and so on. Without looking at the trend (and then the underlying causes), it is very difficult to draw any meaningful conclusions. Yet, that's what newspapers, politicians and companies do regularly. Understanding significance is significant.

- **Regression to the mean:** If you perform well for a period, it will be followed at some point by a drop in performance. If you have great success for a number of years in your career, it will be followed by a dip at some point. It doesn't mean you're no good any more. Second books for authors and movie sequels are often not as good as the original. They are just regression to the mean performance.

- **Filtering:** The average value of a large collection of measurements (say the average number of customer complaints over five years) is about the same as the average value of a large collection (the average number over one year), whereas the extreme value of a large collection (the worst number of complaints over five years) is considerably more extreme than that of a small collection (over one year). So what? Because employers in many sectors usually focus upon winners and extremes, they tend to put people down by comparing them with extraordinary cases ('he's not as good as Wayne Rooney'). In baseball, both the Oakland A's and The Boston Red Sox became highly successful teams by using this insight to their advantage by recruiting players who were perceived by other teams (and therefore overlooked) as average players at knockdown prices. They identified what roles or contributions were inadequate or missing from the team and selected players who had those specific talents even if the rest of their game was ordinary.

What particular hidden talent do you have that employers need, that might have been overlooked by you or others in the past?

▸ **Luck:** In terms of absolute numbers, Paulos says, *"coins behave badly"*. The difference between the number of heads and the number of tails tends to get bigger as we continue to flip the coin, and the changes in lead from head to tail and vice versa tend to become increasingly rare. Unsurprisingly, some people feel like they are losers and others winners, although there is no real difference between them other than luck. So next time you feel sorry for yourself at not getting that dream job or career, remember that you just got stuck on the right (or wrong) side of even.

▸ **Logic:** Paulos argues that faulty logic is a kind of innumeracy. Not being able to conclusively refute a claim does not constitute evidence for them. Think Iraq and WMD. Somewhere in here lies whatever you deem to be informal logic, better known as your common sense. An employer might say you don't have sufficient experience in a particular area. Just because you don't have it written down on your CV, doesn't mean you don't have other relevant experience. One answer is to think more laterally and talk about transferrable skills with examples.

▸ **Decisions:** How you frame a question or statement plays a big role in how someone responds to it. If you were asked how you feel about a 1% cut in your salary, you would probably be more open to that than your reaction to the company announcing a £1 million reduction in the wage bill.

How can you show an employer you have a grasp of numbers and chance? What relevant examples can you provide? How do they support your unique offer for this role, job or employer? How could you present this or articulate it in a way that shows you at your best?

Here are some ideas for you to consider if you struggle with numbers:

▸ Estimate whatever quantity that arouses your interest or the employer's. For example, Karren Brady, Vice-Chair of West Ham United, used an example to demonstrate the relative value of her football club's bid for the Olympic Stadium after 2012 compared with their rivals at Tottenham Hotspur. Spurs' plan was an *"outrageous waste of money"*, the equivalent of *"building more than 100 new primary schools – then bulldozing them after just four weeks"*. Think, 'What I can add to this organisation or save this company is equivalent to...'

▸ Explain it to a friend: talk it through with someone, use them as a sounding board and do a rehearsal with them of how and what you want to say.

▸ Compare a difficult numbers problem with another one that you do understand.

> **Do not worry about your difficulties in Mathematics.
> I can assure you mine are still greater**
>
> Albert Einstein

(The probability of Amy getting the job from the start of the recruitment process is 1 in 191 or 0.5%. Getting an interview at the start is nearly 1 in 30 or 3%. Getting the job before the interview is nearly 1 in 7 or 14%.)

Business and customer awareness

Whichever business you're in or wanting to be in, how well you manage relationships or engage with the company's customers or organisation's users is a fundamental part of being employable. Whatever the effort you put into the other three panes of your window, most employers will judge you ultimately on your contribution to meeting what the customer or service user wants. This includes the quality of both what is delivered and how it is delivered.

The importance of the customer is reflected in one of Marks and Spencer's core values (www.marksandspencer.com), which is about delivering the highest standard of services to their customers:

"Service has perhaps the biggest impact on our people. We want everyone who works for us (no matter what role they're in) to be focused on helping us deliver a service people talk about. This in itself has created a set of values, which apply to all our teams."

Customer service and loyalty is a huge subject that is beyond the scope of this book. In many respects, being effective at the skills, knowledge and attitudes already covered provide a healthy foundation for dealing with customers or users, whether internal or external. Here are some links to the dashboard in Chapter 3:

Positive attitude

Enthusiasm rubs off on the customer or user. What flavour it is will be drawn from your personality, choosing your attitude and enjoying your job. You are the company to the customer and they draw confidence from you. Your self-confidence can come from getting good at what you do and feeling good about yourself.

This is about taking the initiative to resolve a customer's concern, rather than waiting to be asked; taking it on the chin with good grace when they complain because you know how to handle your feelings well; doing what you say you're going to do for a service user; putting forward ideas for new ways to improve the product, service or customer experience; putting yourself forward to make an idea happen so that you are contributing to the whole organisation; and promoting the reputation of the company.

Employers are seeking a mindset whereby employees put themselves in the customer's shoes to see what could make it better. Have you ever been asked to be a mystery shopper, going into the environment where your company engages with the customer? Where could you experience that or something similar? A former colleague used to get paid in his spare time to go into restaurants under cover and rate them.

Self-management

Remember the anecdotes about the IKEA store assistant who took personal responsibility; Amy, the student, who demonstrated her commitment and drive to an employer and got a job against the odds; and Iain, the manager with the construction consultancy, showing the importance of self-starting with both internal and external customers?

In a customer context, it's about knowing when to be assertive and flexible about what the organisation is prepared to do and not do with customers; dealing with difficult behaviours and situations with resilience; ensuring customers reap the benefits of the attention to your health and well-being in the way you communicate and engage with them; turning up on time to service the user and managing your workload so you deliver to the customer; focusing on the 20% of things that make a difference to the user; managing, meeting or exceeding customer expectations; and asking the user what they want/don't want and get/don't get.

It's also about learning from the customer about their wants, needs and concerns; educating and facilitating customers so that, for example, they create their own content or service experience (*"We are defining learning with different people now"* – Jane Bozarth); responding to the learning style of the user, reflecting on the customer experience, questioning assumptions so as to come up with solutions about how to do things better, faster, cheaper.

Align your mindset with the behaviour you want to present to a customer. Remember the anecdote about the check-out staff at the supermarket? Dress in a way that reflects your uniqueness as a person and accords with the expectations of the company and the customer.

Teamworking

Deploy your preferred team contribution so as to be at your best and enhance the customer experience. Lead and follow appropriately depending on the priority given to the organisational value of customer satisfaction. Competing values can sometimes derail the real or intended priority – for example, if internal teamworking is a higher priority in practice than customer satisfaction you can get an inward rather than outward focus at the expense of wider business success.

Co-operate with fellow team members by stepping in to support them where needed and negotiating with or influencing them to reciprocate. Work with and for each other in order to deliver a professional service to the customer or user.

Communication

Ensure your message to users and customers is what you intend, using the media your customers use, want or expect, and targeting the right people. Build rapport by being authentic and genuinely taking an interest in their concerns and connect with people so they warm to your 'personal brand'. Get the customer to think for themselves by asking great questions and, above all, use skilful listening at different levels. Empathise by reflecting on the way you like to do things and then recognising how other people differ, drawing on your personal experiences that may be similar or relevant for your customers. Present your intent verbally and in writing to the customer in a way that recognises their needs and preferences, both in terms of content and how they like to communicate.

Using the internet and social media

Use your understanding of the different ways people are now communicating to tailor your approach to achieving customer satisfaction and loyalty and adapting to generational differences and similarities.

Solving problems

Find innovative solutions to customer or user issues by being creative in a way that suits your strengths and preferences and taking calculated risks through testing things out, and build partnerships with other people and organisations to work collaboratively to resolve problems.

Numeracy

Get basic calculations right when dealing with customers and presenting information accurately to users.

Chapter 7
Making It Stick

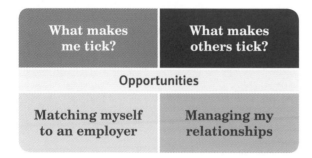

What makes me tick?	What makes others tick?
Opportunities	
Matching myself to an employer	Managing my relationships

We have now reached the final stage of the development process outlined in the book, having explored *Getting it Right* and *Doing it Well*. *Making it Stick* is about maintaining and sustaining your employability through learning and growth and, most importantly, taking action.

How do you make it stick and not get diverted from achieving your goals or dreams? If you give proper attention to the following three elements, you will stand a very good chance of success.

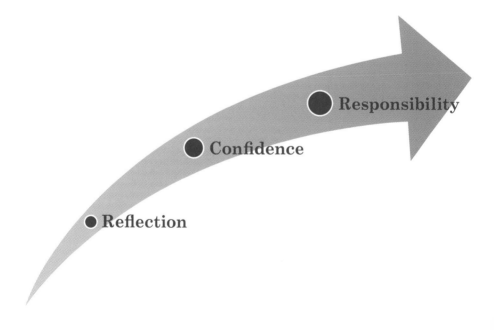

Responsibility

Confidence

Reflection

Developing reflection

In maintaining my employability over many years, I have concluded that deliberate reflection occurs more often as I get older. Self-evidently, I will have done more as time passes. When I was in my twenties, if there was a conscious choice to stop and think, I didn't pay much heed. The more tempting decision was to just dive in and enjoy the moment without looking too far ahead. The current generation seem to have an even more accentuated pull to the present than my generation. Some of this is also about our personalities and the different preferences we have for learning, as we discussed earlier.

The other major change has been the dawn of the Information Age and the increasing speed of change in the world. It doesn't feel like there is time for reflecting. If that's you, how important to you is your goal? You'll find the time and improve your skills in managing how you spend your time if it's important enough to you.

There is also a question mark about how much it is really valued in some organisational cultures. Doing tends to be valued more than thinking. If that's what you face, revisit the question about how well you lead and follow, then take action if necessary. Take the advice of Kate Mercer from the Leadership Lab (http://leaderslab.wordpress.com/):

> *In Buddhism there is a saying, 'don't just do something, sit there'. It's a valuable practice: remain still until you have a grip of what you are facing. Explore your perceptions, challenge their validity, and explore what you really can influence. Remember that for others around you, doing nothing may be perceived as being passive even though you have made a reflective choice. If you choose to 'freeze-frame', put a timeline on it and let people know what you're doing.*

> I would add a third reason to lack of time and cynicism as to the poor status of reflection. Many people don't know how to reflect. Here are some ideas for you to develop your reflective capability in order to be more employable.

▸ Capture your reflections. Find a method that suits you – video diary, audio diary, old-fashioned diary, write a regular blog, tweet. Determine what you will record, how often and when to take stock and review. Then build this habit into your current routine so you get a regular reminder and it pushes you to do it. Periodically, revisit your employability dashboard and capture what is working well for you. Reflect on why you are successful. Break it down bit by bit. For significant events, ask yourself: What do I intend doing/not doing? What did I do? What was the result? What did I learn about myself and others? What surprised or didn't surprise me? What helpful or unhelpful patterns are emerging? What will I continue doing, start doing or stop doing?

▸ Get a coach or a mentor. Find someone on whom you can bounce your ideas, thoughts, feelings, learning and concerns or go to for wise counsel. Look for someone who can provide the right balance of support and challenge for you. You might prefer a formal arrangement but it doesn't have to be one.

▶ Join a community of practice, online or face-to-face. Find like-minded people in your field or who want to learn, reflect on their development, and share ideas and good practices. Coach and mentor one another (See Appendix 1).

▶ Get feedback from other people on how well you are progressing, what you did well, what you could improve.

▶ Develop your reflective capacity by asking yourself great questions and listening to your answers, literally and intuitively. Here are the kind of questions I mean:

- What is the one question you are not asking yourself?
- How do you want to be remembered?
- If you could only earn a living in one way for the rest of your life, what would it be? In light of that, what question would you ask yourself next?
- If your best friend was sitting opposite you, what question would they ask you right now?

Building confidence

Many people lack the confidence to truly explore their potential. Childhood dreams have somehow been forgotten and many ambitions in their youth have long since been sacrificed on the altar of expediency. Regrets are insidious and gnaw away at the soul, as the OPP survey findings of managers in their 40s and 50s illustrated in Chapter 2.

From my experience, the people who are most fulfilled in life are those who are most comfortable in their own skin. They know and like who they are and have an inner confidence and belief in their own abilities irrespective of the circumstances.

They feed that confidence through successes (and promoting them), the right support, giving, and a sense of personal direction and control over their lives. If you want to build that confidence and maintain your employability, consider the wise advice of the late Doug Harvey, a fine colleague, friend and mentor, and be

▶ **consistent** with yourself and who you are
▶ **insistent** by being assertive and proactive
▶ **persistent** and determined in the face of challenges.

Taking personal responsibility for action

In Chapter 4, we explored what a well-rounded learner looked like. It's all very well navel-gazing, I hear some of you say, but you still need to do something to change. This is often the hardest part for many people. We've talked about the self-limiting barriers, personal myths and misassumptions all of us make from time to time. I've also offered a technique to support you in mapping out a plan to achieve your goal or dream. Insight needs to be handcuffed to pragmatic action to increase employability.

Success and fulfilment comes from taking some personal risks, demonstrating our worth to ourselves and others, and building a track record through consistent delivery and achievement in line with our motivational goals, values and beliefs.

I have benefitted from creating my own luck. When one door closed, another one often opened. Make a decision to do X or go to Y and it opens up the possibility of choice, new horizons, ideas and opportunities. Do nothing and you'll get the same again or the environment around you will change without you on board. It's a judgement call.

Procrastination is the woolly comfort blanket of our childhood. It feels safer, yet, at the same time, it scratches. Here are some questions to support and challenge your thinking:

- What do you consistently put off doing?
- What decisions did you avoid this week?
- What have you done today to help make your goal or dream a reality?
- Why don't you already have your dream or goal?
- What would you do if you knew you would never fail?
- Can you think of anything that will stop you from taking your first step?
- Of all the differences that need your attention, what is the one difference, if it were settled, that would make a difference?
- What happens if you do that?
- What happens if you don't do that?
- What doesn't happen if you do that?
- What doesn't happen if you don't do that?

> **Habits, like cactus, are hard to kill. They are like water running downhill; it takes no effort to maintain a habit; even a bad one. Habits are typically rituals that you perform without thinking; they are procedures, to which you are psychologically committed. When your new behaviour is part of a standard procedure that you follow without having to decide each time, you will find that it gets reinforced so that it gradually becomes like that water running downhill**
>
> Shelle Rose Charvet (www.shellestoptips.com)

With your uniqueness comes responsibility, as only you can really decide what is best for you. That attitude of mind and sense of ownership can drive you to take action. Then it's a case of being equipped with skills such as decision-making, planning, implementing and reviewing, and with the knowledge required to support you, such as the tools and approaches in this book. Who am I? What do I want or where am I going? How will I get it or get there? What next?

Doing things differently affects the way you feel. Sometimes, just taking the plunge and seeing how it goes is the right thing to do in a particular circumstance – what Richard Pascale describes as *"acting your way into a new way of thinking, rather than thinking your way into a new way of acting"*. Making the perfect decision can be an illusion. Making poor and good choices, experiencing failures and successes, form what it is to be human and it is from doing so that we get our wisdom. So why fight it?

Chapter 8
Making Each Year a Leap Year

> **Learn from yesterday, live for today, hope for tomorrow.**
> **The important thing is not to stop questioning**
>
> Albert Einstein

I have tried in this book to engage you in a conversation – with yourself. If you walk away from it more impressed with yourself than this book, then I will have succeeded. It has also been about what I believe are some emerging challenges for all of us in being more employable.

I have personally gained interesting insights during the process of researching and writing and they form the content of this last chapter. They are personal reflections and a commentary to prompt your thinking and I look forward to a lively exchange of views if you want to get in touch (see Appendix 1).

The clash between our experience and our expectations

Much of the content of this book is not new, but the context is a complex, changing narrative. The predictions earlier in the decade from the London School of Economics and Demos are proving accurate: we have a more autonomous workplace, more connectivity in society (not just the workplace), and a search for meaning and identity as the world becomes more fragmented, complex and insecure. What we know (knowledge capital), how we use it (technology), what we believe in (values), how we want to organise ourselves (networks) and, above all, relationships, are underpinning this autonomy and connectivity.

The role of trust is crucial as employees get more demanding and the lines between work and non-work get blurred, with greater freedom and flexibility arising from the 'anytime, anywhere' social connectivity driven by technological advances.

In stark terms, our current experience is one of a suffocating economic environment pressing down on our freedom of choice leading to compromise and pragmatism increasingly being the drivers of our options and behaviours for being employable. Finding a job you like and that complements your strengths may be a longer-term goal for some. You may have to take what you can get in the short-term. As an aspiration and a more sustainable route to being fulfilled, the pay-offs make the approaches in this book still worthwhile. Standing out ought not to be about trying to be something you're not. Being authentic can make someone stand out in these reality-show/celebrity-culture-driven times. It remains to be seen how this clash with our expectations will play out over time.

My aim has been to look again at what makes us and others tick, and at how to use that awareness skilfully and authentically to develop and sustain employability in an ever-changing environment. I have used a coaching and mentoring approach to build your awareness, develop your confidence, and encourage ownership and personal responsibility.

> **I cannot teach anybody anything. I can only make them think**
>
> Socrates

Developing coaching and mentoring capability

Early in the book I quoted a manager lamenting the fact he or she had not invested enough in their self-awareness earlier in life. I have met many people in the workplace wanting someone to tell them what to do about the people bit, and how. What does this imply?

It tells us something about how some people are brought up at home, the habits they pick up and take through life, the nature of our education system and the cultures of past and present workplaces.

Sir Ken Robinson is a strong critic of how our educational system operates. *"A degree is not a guarantee anymore, particularly if the route to it marginalises most of the things that you think are important about yourself"*. He believes that we are trying to meet the future by doing what we did in the past and has called for a new paradigm. It is one based on divergent thinking – the ability to see multiple answers rather than one, thinking laterally in finding solutions and ways of interpreting a question. We all have this capacity as children and it mostly deteriorates as we get older. As he explains, you are told at school there is only one answer and it's at the back of the book, don't look or copy – *"once outside of school it's called collaboration"*.

There is a pressing need to move to a different way of educating the next generations. As Einstein wryly observed, *"The only thing that interferes with my learning is my education"*. The philosophy inherent in *Learning to Leap* aligns with Sir Ken's view. A proper balance between coaching and mentoring approaches, rather than instruction and limited freedom for independent thought, would be a step-change in the way we bring our children up at home and school.

As a society, we need to move away from too often stepping in to 'help' when the result is that it infantilises, from being judgemental when the result is loss of self-esteem, from deriding vulnerability when the result is an unhealthy facade, and from over-emphasising shortcomings or weaknesses when the result is being written off too soon or simply not being valued as a person.

At an earlier age, we need to move towards encouraging people to think for themselves within clear boundaries, filling in the gaps where people 'don't know what they don't know', and believing in and nurturing every individual's potential, what Clive Wilson calls 'talent liberation' rather than talent management.

Generational relationships

There are now four generations in the workplace at the same time, which presents both opportunities and challenges for being more employable. These include building effective relationships, resolving conflicts, and making best use of the diversity of skills, experience and values, to name but a few.

Potential does not disappear with age. Learning isn't a chore, although it might have felt like that at times in your life. Part of the reason is that learning to learn has been an undervalued activity. Real experiences, our own or other people's, give us the raw material from which we can genuinely learn. It can be addictive and fun. I believe how someone engages with learning is an indicator of a person's character and maturity, irrespective of their age. I've met 12-year-olds who have been way ahead of their years simply through engaging with reflective learning. I've met 70-year-olds who still want to learn more.

Isn't this a huge opportunity to develop a different kind of workplace that embraces both difference and commonality and brings the generations even closer together? The implications, within and beyond the workplace, are significant; there is the opportunity for greater respect and understanding for who we are as people, rather than for roles and titles, and a real challenge to the notion of hierarchy as we increase our connectedness through networks. Already, we have seen reverse mentoring schemes (such as in the Department for Education) where younger people mentor their seniors on technology or cultural and gender differences.

All this supports my belief that coaching and mentoring mindsets and skills will give you an advantage in standing out from the crowd and enable you to be more employable whether you are in your 60s or your 20s.

Greater self-awareness through knowing the attitudes and values of your own generation, your own patterns of behaviour and what makes you tick, is the first step in being effective in relationships with other generations. You can also develop an understanding of the mindset and behaviours of other generations and then manage yourself skilfully in those interpersonal relations.

So, looking at the older end of the generational spectrum, how is this growing army of experienced, wise and talented people going to excel in the new world order?

Let's take the arts as an example. Both male and female BBC newsreaders of a certain age have already been discarded for younger people, and successful actors find it harder to get roles as they get older, get typecast or end up in Casualty. In contrast, abstract artist Carmen Herrera sold her first painting when she was 89. She now has her paintings exhibited in every major gallery in the world, including the Museum of Modern Art in New York and the Tate Modern.

Was this simply because she was a novelty due to her age or was her creativity and achievement genuinely recognised (or a bit of both)? I think it's more that being visible as you get older is something to do with celebrating your unique wonder as a human being as well as your talent, and continuing to be productive, creative and valued for who you are and what you achieve.

How can society make the paradigm shift from invisibility, condescension and ignorance to visibility, respect and awareness? How do 'older' people stay visible when society often treats them as though they are invisible?

I'll take a bet that a fair proportion of the one million people estimated to lose their jobs in the next five years are likely to face age discrimination in getting a new job, despite new legislation. How prepared are we and can a coaching approach help? Not very prepared, according to a report from the CIPD and the Chartered Management Institute (CMI) which reveals that only 14% of respondents think their employer is prepared for an ageing workforce and few believe they are adequately trained and developed to manage older workers.

Are we sleepwalking into this profound change in our demographics or the *"looming elderquake"*, as the *New York Times* put it. For the first time ever, there are now more people aged over 65 than there are under-fives. The implications for organisations are huge. We are living longer and we will be working longer.

My mother spent some time recently in the critical care ward of a community hospital following a hip operation. She was appalled at the lack of basic respect for the patients – *"patronised, ignored and infantilised"*. Clearly, this isn't the case everywhere, yet we ignore her experience at our peril. When among my teenage children's friends, I also become invisible. Think of this being replicated in the workplace and watch the fireworks.

Research by the Centre on Longevity at Stanford University suggests that the earlier people retire, the quicker their memories decline. Laura L. Carstenson, the Centre's director, says it suggests that *"work actually provides an important component of the environment that keeps people functioning optimally"* and that social and personality skills are also important *(New York Times)*.

We need a mindset change that puts respect and opportunity at the forefront of strategic thinking in employability and people development. *"Governments, industry and international agencies will have to work together to transform the very structure of society, by creating jobs and education programmes for people in their 60s and 70s – the hypothetical middle age"* *(New York Times)*.

How are organisations preparing for 'elderquake'? What incentives are they developing to keep older people working and to benefit from what Carstenson calls these *"wells of expertise"*?

Finding common ground, engaging in the conversation

From my experience, as an unsubstantiated sample of one, the pressure to follow what your parents did or wanted for you was a more common feature of earlier generations than currently. The rise of individualism has led to the mantra of 'choice' in society and less inhibition about deciding what work people want or are prepared to do.

The very notion of a 'career', in the sense of a pre-determined path, is being replaced with a changing set of mini-careers, or 'riding the career carousel' (rather than climbing a ladder) as Ian Gooden of talent management consultancy Chiumento has identified, where you get on and off at various times of your life. This is wonderfully exciting and stimulating for some people, deeply uncomfortable and uncertain for others. Developing and sustaining one's employability is hard and a lifetime's activity.

Many of the current generation have made a paradigm shift in relation to time which affects how they see careers and the world of work. It is based much more on being in the present, living for now. Previous generations have emphasised planning for the future (pensions) and valuing the past (tradition, stability).

Yet, I reflect the dangers of generalising. I believe each generation is moving slowly closer to the next one. Take my three daughters – our musical tastes are much closer than with my parents' generation; we're embracing the technological changes of the era (albeit at a different pace in my case); and here I am, an independent contractor, enterprise/knowledge worker, home-working yet mobile, flexing my hours, building in play, who will probably change directions several times before I retire. Sound familiar? That's how my 22-year-old daughter is talking as she prepares to enter the fray.

The conversation a 22-year-old student has with herself entering the workplace or job market for the first time will have a different tone and focus from a 50-year-old who has found himself redundant. Similarly, 30- and 40-somethings will have a different perspective from 64-year-olds who suddenly find themselves with the opportunity or necessity to carry on working. Yet I hope you will have seen that they have much in common in being more employable.

As long as you have invested in your self-awareness (developed self), you are more likely to have grown beyond your natural-born personality preferences (core self) and engaged productively with different personality types as you age and mature (contextual self). A 50- or 60-year-old may then have an advantage over someone at 30 or 40. If that is you, it's an opportunity for your unique offer to stand out to an employer.

So we're different and the same; let's just keep engaging in this conversation with ourselves and each other to find out what, where, how and why and have fun along the way. This will be critical for all of us in maintaining our employability at whatever stage of our working lives.

The future is collaborative

The opportunity to change the way we learn is within our grasp because of the existential and economic crises society is facing. Our place in the world of work is uncertain and fragile as the foundations of our long-established institutions begin to tremble. It can be a lonely place for individuals.

Most people's experience of learning is as an individual. Learning is about change. The focus of this book has been about aspects of your personal learning and seeking change to be more employable. For me, real-world learning and change involve the power of the collective, as the upheaval in the Arab world in 2011 demonstrated – shared conversations about how we can live and work best together, rather than a passive 'tell me what and how to do it' mentality so readily apparent in many organisations.

A more local example is the work of the Barbican Theatre, Plymouth, who have inspired and engaged school children to reflect on the way they treat other people and the way racism is dealt with through a collaborative theatre project called From One Extreme to the Other. It was commissioned by the local council to challenge attitudes that create racist hatred in secondary schools, community groups, youth clubs etc. As Mark Laville, artistic director, put it: *"Theatre is a powerful catalytic tool for engaging hearts and minds. You can't change behaviour and attitude but you can give people a chance to change it themselves."*

I am not advocating an 'either/or' argument. It's 'and/and' – individual and collaborative. What comes first? Whichever way you look down the telescope, one can inspire the other. Start with collaborative learning and it can inspire the individual. There are plenty of examples in history of inspiring individuals who have moved the masses.

Yet, I believe we have yet to really tap into the empowering effect of the *wisdom of crowds* (James Surowiecki) in our education system as a potentially significant driver for developing and encouraging employability. Some of this has been happening, as my experience of Enterprise Days in schools has illustrated. Unfortunately, the austerity cuts are removing funding and, therefore, posts set up to deliver these primers for growth (for example, at the local Education and Business Partnership in Leeds).

Technological changes, in particular the use of the Internet and the explosion of social media, has created a gap between traditional, formal learning within schools and many organisations and social, informal learning. There are seeds of change in the wind as the work of Jane Bozarth suggests in her book *Social Media for Trainers*. Being more employable in the future is going to include not only getting to grips with social media but learning how to learn with it.

There are plenty of examples emerging. On a global scale, look at the success of TED (Technology, Entertainment and Design), which began as a conference or ideas forum with people like Al Gore speaking, but has now become an online phenomenon. More than 700 TED videoed talks have been put online in the last four years with nearly half a million viewings of a TED talk each day. It has led to TEDx where anybody can hold their own forum if they apply for a licence. According to *The Observer* (23 January 2011), more than 1000 have been held in 80 countries and the newspaper itself held a festival of ideas in March 2011.

This book aims to prompt you to walk (rather than run) at a more modest level in this direction. At Appendix 1, you will find details of how you can join an online learning community on employability. It is designed for you to empower yourself to learn from others, coach and mentor each other and contribute your ideas, questions and resources to anyone with an interest in being more employable.

Never doubt that a small group of thoughtful, committed citizens can change the world. Indeed, it is the only thing that ever has

Margaret Mead, anthropologist

Education, education, education

For me, tomorrow's workplace is a people challenge at its core – how people lead, follow, decide and choose to engage with or respond to the external environment in all its guises. Education (in its broadest sense) is the fundamental building block to creating and taking responsibility for our own future. The CBI has called for employability skills to be part of the national curriculum in schools.

When I was growing up, my dad was fond of the saying *"today is the yesterday of tomorrow"*. It's a variant of Eleanor Roosevelt's quote *"Yesterday is history. Tomorrow is a mystery. Today is a gift. That's why we call it 'The Present'"*. It is echoed by Einstein's quote at the start of this chapter.

And my contribution to these sentiments in Learning to Leap? Make every year a leap year.

Bibliography

Allan, D, Kingdon, M, Murrin, K and Rudkin, D. (2002). *Sticky Wisdom*. Capstone

Ancowitz, N. (2010). 'Introverts and Unemployment – Notes from the Trenches, Part 1', http://selfpromotionforintroverts.com, accessed 11 February 2011

Berens, L V and Nardi D. (2004). *Understanding Yourself and Others: An Introduction to the Personality Type Code*. Telos Publications

Bradberry, T. (2007). *Self-Awareness*. New York: Penguin

Bozarth, J. (2010). *Social Media for Trainers: Techniques for Enhancing and Extending Learning*. San Francisco: Pfeiffer

Buckingham, M and Clifton, D O. (2001). *Now, Discover Your Strengths*. Free Press

Burkeman, O. (2011). *Help! How to Become Slightly Happier and Get a Bit More Done*. Canongate

Chartered Institute of Personnel and Development. (2006). *Managing Organisational Learning & Knowledge*

Chartered Institute of Personnel and Development. (2010). *Soft Skills*

Charvet, S R. (2011). 'Real Behaviour Change: What Does It Take To Break A Habit?'. Article at www.successstrategies.com, accessed 6 January 2011

Christensen, C M. (Jul–Aug 2010). 'How Will You Measure Your Life?'. *Harvard Business Review*

The Confederation of British Industry. (2009). *Future Fit*

Coutu, D L. (May 2002). 'How Resilience Works'. *Harvard Business Review*

Covey, S. (1989). *The Seven Habits of Highly Effective People: Powerful Lessons in Personal Change*. London: Simon and Shuster UK Ltd

Coyle, D. (2009). *The Talent Code*. New York: Bantam

Dunning, D. (2010). *10 Career Essentials: Excel at Your Career by Using Personality Type*. Nicholas Brearley

Dunning, D. (2010, first published in 2001). What's Your Type of Career? *Find Your Perfect Career Using Your Personality Type* (2nd ed). Nicholas Brearley

Frankl, V E. (2004, first published 1946). *Man's Search for Meaning*. Random House

Gallwey, W T. (2004, first published in 1975). *The Inner Game of Tennis*. Pan Books

Garratt, B. (1987). *The Learning Organisation*. Fontana

Goldman, S (ed). (2004). *Mind Game: How the Boston Red Sox Got Smart, Won a World Series, and Created a Blueprint for Winning*. Workman

Goleman, D. (1996). *Emotional Intelligence: why it can matter more than IQ.* London: Bloomsbury

Goleman, D. (2001). *The Emotionally Intelligent Workplace.* Jossey-Bass

Gooden, I. (Jan 2011). *Riding the Career Carousel.* Green Paper from Chiumento

Hanna, J. (20 Sep, 2010). 'Power Posing: Fake it Until You Make it'. *Harvard Business Review*

Holbeche, L. (Oct 2004). *The Power of Constructive Politics.* Roffey Park Institute

Katzenbach, J and Smith D. (2003). *The Wisdom of Teams: Creating the High-Performance Organization.* Harper Collins

Kegan R and Laskow Lehay, L. (1 Nov 2001). 'The Real Reason People Won't Change'. *Harvard Business Review*

Kline, N. (2006). *Time to Think.* Fisher King

Kline, N. (2009). *More Time to Think.* Fisher King

Lawless, J. (2008). *Taming Tigers.* Taming Tigers Publishing

Lencioni, P. (2004). *Death by Meeting.* Jossey-Bass

Lewis, M. (2003). *Moneyball: The Art of Winning an Unfair Game.* New York: W W Norton and Company

Miller, P and Skidmore, P. (2004). *Disorganisation – Why Future Organisations Must 'Loosen Up'.* Demos/Orange

The Mind Gym. (2006). *Give Me Time.* Time Warner

Munz-Jones, N. (2010). *The Reluctant Networker.* HotHive Books

Murray, R M and Rutledge, H. (2009). *Generations: Bridging the Gap with Type.* Performance Consulting/OKA

The Open University. (2010). *Personality and Your Life*

OPP Research. (July 2007). *Dream Job or Career Nightmare*

Pascale, R et al. (Nov–Dec 1997). 'Changing the Way We Change'. *Harvard Business Review*

Paine Schofield, C B and Honore, S. (Winter, 2009). 'Generation Y and Learning'. *360°, The Ashridge Journal*

Paulos, J A. (1990, first published in 1988). *Innumeracy: Mathematical Illiteracy and its Consequences.* Penguin

Pedler, M, Burgoyne, J and Boydell, T. (2007) *A Manager's Guide to Self Development* (5th ed). McGraw-Hill International

Pegg, M. (2008). *The Strengths Toolbox.* Management Books 2000 Ltd

Pierce, V. (2003). *Quick Thinking on Your Feet.* Mercier Press

Pink, D. (2010). 'The Surprising Truth About What Motivates Us'. The Royal Society of Arts. YouTube video at www.theRSA.org, accessed 12 January 2011

Robinson, K. 'Changing Education Paradigms'. The Royal Society of Arts. YouTube video at www.theRSA.org, accessed 12 January 2011

Sinek, S. (2010). *Start with Why: How Great Leaders Inspire Everyone to Take Action.* Portfolio (Penguin)

Sorensen, C. (Nov 2004). *The Future Role of Trust in Work – The Key Success Factor for Mobile Productivity.* LSE/Microsoft

Surowiecki, J. (2004). *The Wisdom of Crowds: Why the Many Are Smarter Than the Few and How Collective Wisdom Shapes Business, Economies, Societies and Nations.* Random House

Taylor, B. (2003). *Forging the Future Together, Human Relations in the 21st Century.* Oasis

The UK Commission for Employment and Skills. (July 2010). *Ambition 2020:World Class Skills and Jobs for the UK*

Wilson, C. (2010). *Talent Liberation.* Primeast

Yeung, R. (2008). *Confidence.* Pearson Education

Zimbardo, P. (2007). *The Lucifer Effect: How Good People Turn Evil.* Rider

Appendix 1
Workbook and Online Learning Community

The *Learning to Leap* Workbook

You can obtain a FREE workbook containing the exercises and activities in the book as a practical tool to support you in taking responsibility for action.

The Employability Hub

You can join the Employability Hub, which has been set up to support the publication of *Learning to Leap*. The aim is to inspire people to be more employable through building a vibrant online learning community, based on its members coaching and mentoring each other. It's for readers of this book and anyone with an interest in employability issues.

Open, inclusive and collaborative, inspiring, creative and practical – you can shape it through your interests and priorities.

I would love to hear from you through the Employability Hub with stories of how you have used *Learning to Leap* to develop and sustain your employability so we can continue our conversation.

Go to **www.employabilitycoaching.co.uk/resources** and leave your details in order to obtain the workbook and join the Employability Hub.

Appendix 2
Personality Assessments

Instrument	What's it about?	Why use it?
The Myers-Briggs Type Indicator www.opp.eu.com	The MBTI was developed by mother and daughter team, Katherine Briggs and Isabel Briggs-Myers and is based on the work of psychologist Dr Carl Jung in the 1920s. The questionnaire has been around since the 1970s and is used by millions worldwide. It categorises people into four personality 'types' – mental frameworks that inform what we prefer doing rather than our ability to do them. Certain patterns of behaviour may indicate the mental framework from which someone is coming. So our starting point is from a particular 'type' but we can move to other ones if we choose. The more we develop aspects of these less-preferred types, the more we can see things from other people's perspectives and see how to manage those relationships where we differ. The MBTI focuses on how people like to take in information and make decisions. It helps explain why some people are more energised by other people and situations whereas some prefer to think things through before expressing an opinion, why some people like detail and others a broader picture, and why some people prefer a systematic, planned approach to life rather than a more spontaneous one. Only 3–12% of people will be similar in their approach and no one is exactly the same as you. This not about 'putting people into boxes'. As careers and personality expert, Donna Dunning, says *"these preferences do not dictate how people act. People can choose their preferred or non-preferred ways of acting to respond to situations. Personality type provides a flexible, positive approach to individual differences"*.	▶ Online or paper-based completion, in-depth reports from accredited practitioner (cost involved) on overall type, communications, problem solving and decision-making. ▶ For an in-depth understanding of how you and others see the world from your hilltops, the implications for how you and they then choose to act or behave (or not). ▶ For recognising that different types are a worthwhile lens through which to view people. ▶ For recognising that different types bring added value to our own view of the world. ▶ It is a common language in the workplace, as so many people have taken the MBTI.

Instrument	What's it about?	Why use it?
IDISC www.personality code.com	Also in use by millions of people around the world over the last 30 years, this is based on behaviour traits (actually what we do rather than mental frameworks) and the work of Dr William Marston in the 1920s. He described four predominant behaviour patterns – active and task-oriented, active and people-oriented, reactive and task-oriented, reactive and people-oriented. It identifies which of 14 personality profiles, based on the four behavioural traits, best fits you.	▸ Completing the online questionnaire takes 15 minutes. ▸ You get access to e-learning materials to help you make sense of/get the best out of your profile.
Strength Deployment Inventory http://uk.personal strengths.com	The SDI is based on Relationship Theory and the work of Dr Elias Porter and Carl Rogers in the 1930s. It has four premises: ▸ We all do what we do because we want to feel good about ourselves ▸ We tend to take two different approaches to life – when we feel things are going well and when we feel that we are faced with opposition or conflict ▸ A 'personal weakness' is no more than the overdoing or misapplying of a personal strength ▸ We naturally tend to perceive the behaviours of others through our own. The SDI is a learning model that is helpful for understanding the motives behind your behaviour. Each person has a *Motivational Value System*, which is the basis for which a person seeks to be valued, by self, others and in all life situations. When we take on board the MVS of others we can learn to relate to each other in more effective ways. It also helps to explain and predict how we tend to deal with conflict by understanding our own approach, so allowing us to manage it more effectively, recognise the signs early in others and move away from our own preferred style to another which could be more effective.	▸ Online or paper-based completion and facilitated feedback with an accredited practitioner. ▸ For understanding the motives behind behaviour – what drives you and other people. ▸ Gives you a portrait of your strengths and overused strengths. ▸ For explaining and predicting your likely response to dealing with conflict. ▸ It differs from but complements the MBTI. Some people remember their preference better because the SDI uses colours (rather than a code like MBTI).

Instrument	What's it about?	Why use it?
Saville WAVE Work-based Styles www.saville consulting.com	Introduced more recently, and heavily researched, the questionnaire measures work styles based on a model about performance and potential (WAVE). It is not a personality questionnaire but a work-based styles one. Explores your motives, preferences, needs and talents in critical work areas, ie the relationship between what you enjoy and what you are good at. Looks at four clusters – thought, influence, adaptability and delivery.	▸ Online completion and in-depth report provided by accredited practitioner on work styles and competency potential. ▸ Combines assessment of personality, motivation, competency and culture rather than as separate instruments. ▸ Helps you understand the culture where you can thrive. ▸ Helps predict your job performance. ▸ Helps identify where there is/is not alignment between what you enjoy and what you are good at.
Interpersonal Dynamics Inventory Contact alison@ alisonmilne.co.uk	The IDI is a 360-degree instrument based on Social Style Theory originating from the 1960s. It measures a person's 'social style' based on the view that individuals tend to exhibit habitual patterns of behaviour in what they say and do (Directiveness), how they relate to people (Affiliation), and how they perform tasks or process information (Adaptability). The focus here is on observable behaviours that can be described by others, not how you think or feel. The IDI describes four styles of behaviour that others can see, each with strengths and weaknesses – Motivators, Relators, Processors and Producers.	▸ Online completion and in-depth report provided by accredited practitioner (cost involved). ▸ Requires six other people to complete a questionnaire on how they see you behave. ▸ Helps you develop better relationships with others. ▸ Strong relationship between the styles and how people behave in a conflict situation.

Instrument	What's it about?	Why use it?
Finding Potential www.finding potential.com	This one is very recent, generic, based on the 'Big Five' personality traits: ▸ **Openness** indicates how willing we are to explore new ideas and ways of doing things. ▸ **Conscientiousness** indicates how well we plan and exhibit self-control. ▸ **Extroversion** indicates our desire for stimulation. ▸ **Agreeableness** indicates how easily we get along with others. ▸ **Neuroticism** indicates how we deal with negative emotions such as stress and anxiety.	▸ Free and can be completed online in 15 minutes, quick and easy to use with an instant downloadable report. ▸ Downloadable, practical workbooks on Making the Most of Your Personality Profile, Employment Career Choices, How to Be At Your Best in a Team, all in plain English.
Entrepreneur Scan www. entrepreneur scan.co.uk Contact Dan@ entrepreneur scan.co.uk	E-Scan, as it is known, is a relatively new profiling tool, originally from the Netherlands where it has been widely adopted. It is based upon scientific research measuring the calibre of budding entrepreneurs against the competencies and characteristics of successful entrepreneurs. The E-Scan analyses a person's characteristics and thinking styles, resulting in an entrepreneurial profile, or 'Entrepreneurial DNA', which provides an objective view on how their capabilities compare to those who are most successful as businesspeople.	▸ Free completion and downloadable summary report (a more in-depth one has a cost). ▸ Helps entrepreneurs understand their own strengths and weaknesses to enable better business performance. ▸ Also useful in exploring how people work, how they process new ideas and products, areas where they might need to consider bringing in specialist help to cover gaps or weaknesses in their skill set.

Instrument	What's it about?	Why use it?
BBC's Child of Our Time 2010 Big Personality Test www.bbc.co.uk/labuk/experiments/personality	Dr Jason Rentfrow of the University of Cambridge says *"BBC Lab UK's Big Personality Test aims to answer the question – do our personalities shape our lives or do our lives shape our personalities? More than a quarter of a million people have taken the test since it launched in November 2009, making this the largest ever scientific study of personality in Britain. At the core of the Big Personality Test are the 'Big Five' personality traits. Everyone exhibits these five traits to a greater or lesser degree, which allows psychologists to build up a sort of 'personality fingerprint' that can be used as a point of comparison between individuals."*	▸ Free, broad-brush approach, quick online completion, instant results, not in-depth. ▸ You can make a broad comparison with those who have completed it.

You will need the support of an accredited or licensed practitioner in interpreting your profile if using MBTI, SDI, Saville Wave and IDI. This is not essential for IDISC, Finding Potential and E-Scan, although a professional coach with whom to talk it through is recommended. Some good sources are the Coaching and Mentoring Network (www.coachingnetwork.org.uk) and the Coaching at Work coach members' list (www.coaching-at-work.com).